Present Value Applications for Accountants and Financial Planners

Recent Titles from Quorum Books

Present Value Applications for Accountants and Financial Planners

G. Eddy Birrer
and
Jean L. Carrica

QUORUM BOOKS
New York • Westport, Connecticut • London

Library of Congress Cataloging-in-Publication Data

Birrer, G. Eddy.
    Present value applications for accountants and financial planners
/ G. Eddy Birrer and Jean L. Carrica.
       p.   cm.
    Includes index.
    ISBN 0-89930-307-2 (lib. bdg. : alk. paper)
    1. Business mathematics. 2. Present value analysis. I. Carrica,
Jean L. II. Title
    HF5695.B53   1990
    657–dc20   89-10218

British Library Cataloguing in Publication Data is available.

Library of Congress Catalog Card Number: 89-10218
ISBN: 0-89930-307-2

First published in 1990 by Quorum Books

Greenwood Press, Inc.
88 Post Road West, Westport, Connecticut 06881

Printed in the United States of America

∞

The paper used in this book complies with the
Permanent Paper Standard issued by the National
Information Standards Organization (Z39.48–1984).

10 9 8 7 6 5 4 3 2 1

Contents

90-2124

Tables

Preface

The primary subject of this book is the application of present value concepts and techniques to individual and business decisions involving future cash flows. Emphasis is placed on developing clear presentations of topics, supplemented by readily understood examples and cash flow illustrations, providing a logical framework for completing more in-depth analyses.

The authors have chosen to focus on concepts and techniques throughout the book rather than on the use of specific calculators or computer software packages available for use in making present value calculations. We believe that given the framework for making present value analyses, readers will have a better grasp of various concepts and techniques and when each should be applied. Nonetheless, readers are encouraged to use calculators and computers to support the decision-making process.

Acknowledgments

The authors wish to thank the National Association of Accountants for permission to use their published tables of present and future time value of money factors as an appendix to this book. We extend our gratitude to Teri Stroschein for her tireless work in typing the manuscript and preparing related tables. We also appreciate the patience and support of our families as we completed work on the book.

Present Value Applications for
Accountants and Financial Planners

1

Overview of Present Value
Concepts and Techniques

Individuals and businesses regularly make decisions that have direct financial implications to them. They must make choices between investments in one corporate stock or another, cash rebates or reduced interest rate financing offered by automobile manufacturers, and fixed rate or adjustable rate mortgages among other choices. Businesses have to determine whether an equipment acquisition will be profitable. Individuals must decide how to accumulate funds for education or retirement. This book introduces present value concepts and techniques useful in making decisions involving choices of these types.

Many accountants, financial managers, and personal financial planners have become aware of the importance of a thorough understanding of time value of money concepts and their application in personal and business financial planning and decision making. Accountants incorporate present value calculations into the valuation of leases, bonds, and other financial statement items. Financial managers use present value techniques for capital budgeting and other decisions. Personal financial planners, both within and outside the accounting profession, are becoming increasingly aware of the usefulness of present value analysis in serving clients. Eugene F. Brigham, author of *Financial Management: Theory and Practice,* cites the time value of money as the most important technique used in finance.

TIME VALUE OF MONEY CONCEPT

The value of a dollar today is normally greater than that of a dollar receivable or payable at a later date, for at least two reasons: (1) in periods of inflation, a dollar loses its purchasing power, so a dollar can be used to purchase more goods or services today than a year hence; and (2) a dollar held today can be invested to earn interest or some other return. For example, a dollar invested today at 6 percent interest will have a value at the end of one year of $1.06, thereby making it worth more than a dollar received at the end of that year.

Time value of money analysis, hereafter referred to generally as present value analysis, builds on this basic concept: that a dollar held today is worth more than a dollar received in the future. There exist a variety of applications of this elementary concept that often require sophisticated analyses. Effective use of present value techniques requires specifying the timing of cash flows, determining what is appropriately included in cash flow amounts, identifying an interest or discount rate for measuring the value of cash flows, and determining whether the present value or the future value of the cash flows should be calculated.

PRESENT VALUE AND FUTURE VALUE CALCULATIONS

Throughout this book reference will be made to present value (PV) and future value (FV) calculations, although emphasis is placed on PV analysis.

Future Value of 1

In some cases it is necessary to determine the value in the future of a single amount deposited (invested) today and left on deposit until some future date. For example, one may want to determine the value at the end of five years of $10,000 deposited today in a savings account that provides simple annual interest of 6 percent. The following time line illustrates the cash flow in this example:

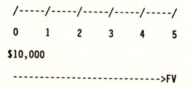

```
/-----/-----/-----/-----/-----/
0     1     2     3     4     5

$10,000

---------------------------->FV
```

The general equation used to solve the problem is $X \ an/i = FV$, where

$X is the amount deposited,
  a represents the future value of a *single* amount,
  n represents the number of interest periods,
  i represents the interest rate, and
FV is the future value of the amount in question.

In the example the equation becomes $10,000 $a5/6$ = FV. The "Future Value of $1" table in the Appendix can be used to solve the equation. By referring to the period 5 line under the 6 percent column, you will see the factor 1.338, which is substituted for $a5/6$ in the equation, as follows: ($10,000) (1.338) = FV = $13,380. Therefore the value at the end of Year 5 of $10,000 deposited today and left to accumulate at 6 percent simple interest is $13,380.

This table also can be used to calculate the amount that must be deposited today so that a specific amount will be available at a future date. Assume that an individual would like to have $4,000 available at the end of three years in a fund that earns 10 percent simple interest. Using $X for the unknown amount, the amounted deposited, and $4,000 for FV, the desired future value, the equation to be solved is $X $a3/10$ = $4,000. Using the factor 1.331 in place of $a3/10$, the equation becomes ($X) (1.331) = $4,000. Solving for $X, the amount to be deposited today to accumulate to $4,000 at the end of three years at 10 percent is $3,005.

Any future value of 1 problem can be solved by substituting known amounts into the general equation $X an/i = FV and solving for the one unknown amount, regardless of whether it is the deposit, interest rate, time period, or future value.

Future Value of an Ordinary Annuity of 1

An annuity problem exists when one wants to make equal periodic deposits over time rather than a single deposit at the beginning of the first period. The general equation used to solve for the future value of an ordinary annuity is $X An/i = FV, where

$X is the amount to be deposited at the end of each period,
  A indicates future value of an annuity (equal periodic deposits),
  n represents the number of periodic deposits,
  i represents the rate of interest that will be earned, and
FV is the future value.

To determine the accumulated future value of a series of equal deposits of $1,000 made at the end of each year for six years at 8 percent interest, refer to the "Future Value of an Ordinary Annuity of $1" table in the Appendix. The following time line illustrates the cash flows in the example:

```
/-----/-----/-----/-----/-----/-----/
0     1     2     3     4     5     6

   $1000 $1000 $1000 $1000 $1000 $1000

----------------------------------->FV
```

The equation used to solve the problem in this case is $1,000 A6/8 = FV. Refer to the period 6 line under the 8 percent column in the table, and you will find the time value factor 7.336. The equation then becomes ($1,000) (7.336) = FV = $7,336, the value at the end of Year 6 of equal annual deposits of $1,000 compounded at 8 percent simple interest.

The table assumes that cash flows occur at the end of each period, whereas the "Future Value of $1" table assumed that the cash flow occurred at the beginning of the first period. Other problems involving the future value of an annuity can also be solved using the general equation of $X An/i = FV. Frequently the desired future value is known, and the equal periodic deposit is to be determined. Other cases require determining the interest rate or time periods necessary to achieve certain fund accumulations. Such problems can be solved if only one variable in the equation is unknown. If cash flows occur at the beginning of each period, an annuity due factor (discussed later in the chapter) is used.

Present Value of 1

Calculations requiring determination of the value today of amounts received in the future are referred to as present value or discounted cash flow calculations. The general equation used to determine the present value of a single amount is $X pn/i = PV, where

$X is the amount to be received in the future,
 p indicates present value of a single future amount,
 n is the number of periods hence to the receipt,
 i is the interest rate to be used in discounting the future cash flow, and

PV represents the present value (the value today of the cash received in the future).

To illustrate, assume that the amount one must receive today to be just as well off as receiving $10,000 five years from today is to be determined. Further, assume any amount held today can be invested at 8 percent interest. The time line representing the cash flow pattern and the desired calculation follows:

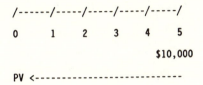

In this case the equation becomes $10,000 $p5/8 = PV$. Refer to the "Present Value of $1" table in the Appendix to find the factor .681 on the period 5 line under the 6 percent column. Substituting .681 for $p5/8$, the equation becomes ($10,000) (.681) $= PV = $6,810$. Therefore an individual receiving $10,000 five years hence is just as well off as one who receives $6,810 today. Note that the present value of a single future receipt or payment is the reverse of that for the future value of 1. This can be proved by multiplying $6,810 by the future value of 1 factor for five periods at 8 percent: $6,810 $a5/8 = FV = ($6,810) (1.469)$ = $10,004 (off $4 because table factors are rounded to three places). Any part of the equation can be determined so long as only one item is unknown.

Present Value of an Annuity of 1

Many present value analyses require determination of the value today of a series of equal payments or receipts due at the end of each of several periods. The concept is the reverse of that which applies to calculations of the future value of an annuity. The general equation used for stating such problems is $X $Pn/i = PV,$ where

$X is the equal periodic receipt or payment at the end of each period,
  P indicates calculation of the present value of an annuity (instead of a single amount),
  n is the number of time periods over which cash flows will occur,

i is the appropriate rate for discounting cash flows, and
PV represents the value today of the future cash flows.

Assume an investment provides for annual cash inflows of $600 at the end of each year for the next four years and that such investments should provide a return of 12 percent. To understand determination of the amount that should be paid for the investment, it is helpful to draw the following time line to depict the cash flows and the desired calculation:

```
/-----/-----/-----/-----/
0     1     2     3     4

    $600  $600  $600  $600

PV <---------------------
```

The problem can then be stated in equation form: $600 \, P4/12 = PV$. By referring to the "Present Value of an Ordinary Annuity of $1" table, you can find the factor 3.037 on the period 4 line under the 12 percent column. Substituting this factor for $P4/12$, the equation becomes ($600) (3.037) = PV = $1,822. That is, an investor desiring a 12 percent return would be willing to pay $1,822 for the investment. Note that this is $578 less than the cash received from the investment ($2,400 − $1,822); the difference represents the 12 percent interest return.

As with the other general equations, the present value of an annuity equation can be used to solve for any of the variables in the equation provided there is only one unknown. Most of the topics covered in this book require use of the present value of an annuity equation. Note that in cases where cash flows occur at the beginning of each period, an annuity due factor must be used to calculate present values.

Future Value of an Annuity Due of 1

The "Future Value of an Ordinary Annuity of $1" table assumes that cash flows occur at the end of each time period. Some cases, however, require determining the future value of equal periodic cash flows occurring at the beginning of each period. This cash flow pattern is referred to as an *annuity due* rather than an ordinary annuity. Calculation of its amount is made by adjusting the factor in the "Future Value of an Ordinary Annuity" table to reflect that deposits or payments occur at the beginning of each period. The general equation is $X \, Adn+1/i − 1.000 = FV$ where

X is the equal periodic receipt or payment at the beginning of each period,

Ad indicates calculation of the future value of an annuity due,

$n+1$ is the number of time periods over which cash flows will occur plus 1 to reflect earnings on the first year's cash flows,

i is the appropriate interest rate for compounding interest, and

-1.000 is an adjustment to the ordinary annuity factor to reflect that the cash flows occur for only n periods.

To illustrate, the value at the end of Year 4 of an annuity due of $5,000 per year compounded at 10 percent interest is to be determined. The following time line illustrates the problem:

```
/-------/-------/-------/-------/
 0       1       2       3       4

$5,000   $5,000  $5,000  $5,000

----------------------------> FV
```

Solution of the problem requires adjusting the future value of an ordinary annuity factor to reflect that the first cash flow earns interest during the first year (which it does not in an ordinary annuity). This is done by using the factor for $n+1$ periods for the extra year of compounding and then subtracting 1.000 to account for the fact that the cash flows occur for only n periods. Using the facts given, the equation to depict the cash flows is $5,000 $Ad4+1/10 - 1.000 = FV$. From the table, the period 5 (4+1) factor is 6.105. Subtracting 1.000 gives 5.105. The equation then becomes ($5,000) (5.105) = FV = $25,525. (Separate tables of annuity due factors are available for those who must solve a variety of such problems without the use of a calculator or a computer.)

Present Value of an Annuity Due of 1

The present value of an ordinary annuity table can also be adjusted to reflect cash flows at the beginning of each period. The adjustment requires use of the present value factor for $n-1$ periods to reflect the fact that the cash flow at the beginning of period 1 does not need to be discounted. However, 1.000 is added to the factor to account for the cash flow that occurs at the beginning of the first period. The general equation for the present value of an annuity is therefore modified to appear as

follows for the calculation of the present value of an annuity due: $X
$Pdn{-}1/i + 1.000 = PV$, where

> $X   is the equal periodic receipt or payment at the beginning of each
>   period,
> Pd indicates calculation of the present value of an annuity due
>   (remember that P represents calculation of the present value of
>   an ordinary annuity),
> $n{-}1$ is the number of time periods over which cash flows will occur
>   minus 1 to reflect the fact that the first year's earnings need not
>   be discounted,
> i is the appropriate interest rate for compounding interest, and
> $+1.000$ is an adjustment to the ordinary annuity factor to reflect the
>   cash flow occurs at the beginning of the first period.

For example, assume that the present value of a stream of cash flows
of $8,000 received at the beginning of each year for five years is to be
determined and that an appropriate interest rate is 9 percent. The cash
flows and related calculation are illustrated in the following time line:

```
/--------/-------/-------/-------/-------/
0        1       2       3       4       5

$8,000   $8,000  $8,000  $8,000  $8,000

PV <---------------------------------------
```

The modified equation for the present value of an annuity due in this case
is $8,000 $Pd5{-}1/9 + 1.000 = PV$. The period 4 line $(5 - 1)$ factor under
the 9 percent column in the "Present Value of an Ordinary Annuity of $1"
table is 3.240. Adding 1.000 to reflect the beginning of Year 1 cash flow
that is not discounted, the factor becomes 4.240. Substituting the factor
into the equation, ($8,000) (4.240) = PV = $33,920.

An alternative but essentially similar approach to solving the problem
is simply to add $8,000 to the present value of the last four payments.
Because the last four payments constitute an ordinary annuity, the
solution becomes $8,000 + $8,000 $P4/9 = PV = $8,000 + ($8,000)
(3.240) = $33,920. The advantage of this approach is that there is no
need to remember how to adjust present value factors for annuities due.
Of course, an annuity due table could be obtained, or a calculator or
computer could be used to make this calculation.

Lease payments, automobile and mortgage payments, and a variety of other financing and investing receipts and payments schedules can require the use of annuity due calculations.

Other Present and Future Value Tables

The use of present value calculations is so extensive that specialized tables have been prepared for several industries. Most readers are familiar with loan books used by banks and other financial institutions that show periodic payment amounts under a variety of repayment and interest terms. Specialized tables are also available in the real estate industry. Some publications include annuity due tables and tables with cash flows assumed to occur uniformly throughout each period. The various tables are developed using the concepts presented in this book and are not presented separately; however, readers may find it helpful to obtain one or more of these specialized books of tables and values.

Summary of Notation Used in the Book

The equations used in this book for solving present and future value case problems relate to the four tables in the Appendix. Following is a summary of the equations pertaining to each table and used for solving related problems:

Future Value of 1 ($X $an/i = FV$): Used to determine the future value of a single given sum, a, at the end of n periods at compound interest rate i.

Future Value of Ordinary Annuity of 1 ($X $An/i = FV$): Used to determine the accumulated future value of a series of equal deposits, A, made each period for n periods and compounded at i interest.

Present Value of 1 ($X $pn/i = PV$): Used to determine the value now of a single given sum, p, due n periods hence, discounted at compound interest rate i.

Present Value of an Ordinary Annuity of 1 ($X $Pn/i = PV$): Used to determine the value now of a series of equal amounts, P, due each period for n periods, discounted at compound interest rate i.

In addition, the equation $X $Adn+1/i - 1.000$ was developed for calculating the future value of an annuity due, and $X $Pdn-1/i$ was developed for calculating the present value of an annuity due.

ADDITIONAL PROBLEMS IN COMPLETING
PRESENT VALUE ANALYSES

This chapter so far has dealt with straightforward calculations of present and future values assuming equal periodic cash flows and annual interest compounding problems. Further, all cash flows were related to time periods beginning with Year 1. However, there exist a variety of circumstances when such direct calculations cannot be made.

Interest Compounding Periods of
Other Than One Year

Monthly, quarterly, semiannual, and other compounding periods are easily dealt with in completing present value analyses. Each case requires that table factors selected for solving problems reflect time periods of other than one year. In fact, each line in the present and future value tables represents a time period of any length — not necessarily one year. And the interest columns represent interest rates for individual time periods regardless of length. Therefore, a problem involving quarterly compounding at 8 percent annual interest for five years would require use of the factor for twenty periods (5 years x 4 quarters per year) at 2 percent (8 percent annual interest ÷ 4 quarters). Thus the future value of $10,000 invested today for five years at 8 percent annual interest compounded quarterly would be expressed by the following equation: $10,000 \ a20/2 = FV = (\$10,000) \ (1.486) = \$14,860$. The 1.486 factor is taken from the period 20 line under the 2 percent column of the "Future Value of $1" table. Note that annual compounding of interest would have resulted in a future value of only $14,690 ($10,000 x the 5 year, 8 percent factor of 1.469) because there is no compounding of interest within each year.

In summary, the appropriate time period and percentage table factor is found by multiplying the time period by two, four, twelve, and so on, depending on whether the respective compounding period is semiannual, quarterly, monthly, and so on, and by dividing the annual interest rate by two, four, and so on, depending on the number of compounding periods in the year.

Deferred Payments or Annuities

In some cases, cash flows commence after one or more years, requiring exercise of additional care when using present and future value tables. Recall that the "Future Value of $1" table assumes that an amount is deposited at the beginning of Year 1 and that the "Present Value of $1" table assumes a single future amount to be discounted to the value at the beginning of period 1. The annuity tables assume that cash flows occur at the end of each period beginning with the first time period. If cash flows do not coincide with theassumptions made when the table factors were developed, it is necessary to adjust calculations.

Assume, for example, that the present value of four equal receipts of $7,000 is to be determined and that the receipts occur at the end of each of Years 4–7. The interest rate is 10 percent. A time line depicting the cash flows and the calculation to be made follows:

```
/-------/-------/-------/-------/-------/-------/-------/

0       1       2       3       4       5       6       7

                                $7,000  $7,000  $7,000 $7,000

PV <---------------------------------------------------------
```

Note that discounting $7,000 for seven periods will overstate the solution because the cash flows occur in only four periods. Further, use of the Year 4, 10 percent factor will also overstate the solution because there is no discounting of the cash flows during the three-year deferral period. Two approaches for dealing with these problems will be considered.

First, the $7,000 annuity can be discounted to its present value at the end of Year 3 using the period 4, 10 percent factor contained in the "Present Value of an Annuity of $1" table (Year 3 is time zero). The present value amount at the end of Year 3 can then be discounted to the beginning of Year 1 using the period 3, 10 percent factor contained in the "Present Value of $1" table. In equation form, the solution is ($7,000 $P4/10$) ($p3/10$) $= PV$. Substituting table factors, the equation becomes [($7,000) (3.170)] [.751] $= PV =$ [$22,190] [.751] $= $16,665$.

A second approach to solving the problem is to refer only to the "Present Value of an Annuity of $1" table. Under this approach the period 7, 10 percent factor is reduced by the period 3, 10 percent factor to account for the fact that there are no cash flows the first three years. Expressed in equation form, the solution is ($7,000) ($P7/10 - P3/10$) $= PV =$ ($7,000) (4.868 − 2.487) $=$ ($7,000) (2.381) $= $16,667$ (the answer differs by $2 from that obtained using the first approach because table factors are rounded to three places). Because both approaches produce the same answer, the choice of which to use is left to the reader.

Uneven Cash Flows

Calculation of the present or future value of a stream of cash flows can become cumbersome when periodic cash flows are not constant in amount. Calculations are further complicated if payments are deferred beyond one time period. Use of a time line to depict cash flows becomes even more important in those cases if present or future value calculations are to be made correctly. Preparation of a time line should make apparent how to solve a present or future value analysis problem. In some cases, the present or future value of each cash flow amount will have to be calculated separately and the individual solutions summed to determine an answer. In other cases, there will be a mixture of individual and annuity cash flows whose present and future value are to be calculated.

To illustrate, assume that the present value of cash flows depicted in the following time line is to be determined. Assume cash flows occur at the end of each year and that the discount rate is 12 percent:

```
/-------/-------/-------/-------/-------/-------/
0       1       2       3       4       5       6

     $1,000  $1,000  $3,000  $3,000  $3,000  $3,000

PV <--------------------------------------------
```

The time line illustration shows that there are two annuity streams in this case. There are several approaches to solving this problem. The most direct is to calculate the present value of an ordinary annuity of $3,000 for six years at 12 percent and then to deduct the present value of an ordinary annuity of $2,000 for two years (Years 1 and 2 when the cash flows were $1,000, not $3,000 — that is, a $2,000 difference). In equation form, the solution is ($3,000 $P6/12$) − ($2,000 $P2/12$) = PV = [($3,000) (4.111)] − [($2,000) (1.690)] = $12,333 − $3,380 = $8,953. Alternatively the present value could be determined by discounting each of the six cash flows using present value of 1 factors and then summing the respective amounts. Another approach is to discount the ordinary annuity of $1,000 for the first two years and add that amount to the present value of the deferred annuity of $3,000, calculated using one of the two approaches discussed on deferred annuities. The best approach to follow in a given case is a function of the timing, amounts, and frequency of the various cash flows.

Solving for an Implicit or Unknown Interest Rate

If all variables but one are known in the general equations provided for solving each type of present or future value problem, the unknown variable can be determined. In some cases, however, it may be necessary to use an estimated market rate or to impute interest using an estimate of the fair value of an item acquired. Determining the interest rate implicit in a given financial arrangement may require trial-and-error computations when cash flows are uneven in amount. Here we look at examples that illustrate the calculation of implicit rates of interest. (Note that in Chapters 3 and 4, reference is made to internal rate of return, or IRR. The implicit rate and IRR are the same.)

Assume that a three-year noninterest-bearing note for $4,000 is exchanged for an item of equipment worth $3,176. To determine the interest rate implicit in the note, it is necessary to discount the $4,000 to a present value of $3,176, as illustrated by the following time line:

```
/-------/-------/-------/

0       1       2       3

                        $4,000

PV <----------------------

PV=$3,176
```

The equation for calculating the present value of 1 is $4,000 $p3/i = PV = $3,176. The $p3/i$ factor is determined by dividing $3,176 by $4,000. The $p3/i$ factor is computed to be .794. If you refer to the period 3 line in the "Present Value of $1" table, you will find .794 under the 8 percent column. Thus, 8 percent is the rate of interest implicit in the noninterest-bearing note.

As another example, assume that machinery with a fair market value of $30,000 is acquired from a dealer under a lease agreement requiring a $5,000 payment at the inception of the lease and payments at the end of each year for ten years in the amount of $4,068, as depicted in the following time line:

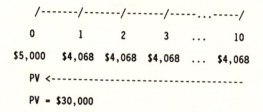

```
       /-------/-------/-------/-----...-----/
       0       1       2       3    ...   10
     $5,000  $4,068  $4,068  $4,068  ...  $4,068
       PV <-------------------------------------
       PV = $30,000
```

After the initial payment on the lease, $25,000 of the machinery value remains to be financed under the lease arrangement. The interest rate is determined by discounting the remaining cash flows to the present value of the amount financed. The equation is $4,068 $P10/i = PV = $25,000$. The $P10/i$ factor is 6.145 ($25,000 ÷ $4,068) and is found under the 10 percent column on the period 10 line. Therefore, the rate of interest implicit in the lease is 10 percent.

If the fair market value of the equipment is not readily determinable, its value has to be estimated using an assumed interest rate. The rate should approximate that charged by lenders for a similar financing arrangement, often referred to as the *incremental borrowing rate*. If, for example, the purchaser expected to pay 9 percent for additional (incremental) financing, then the lease payments would be discounted at that rate. The present value of the payments plus the $5,000 down payment would be used as an indication of the value of the equipment.

The preceding examples were designed to result in factors that can be found directly in the present value tables. Often, however, the factor calculated using the equations will not appear in the related table. This is especially likely in situations involving uneven or irregular cash flows. In those cases it is necessary to calculate the implicit rate through the process of interpolation.

Interpolation

Two examples will be used to illustrate interpolation: a case requiring determination of the rate implicit in a problem with a single future cash flow and a case involving uneven cash flows. Assume in the first case that the implicit interest rate is to be determined for an investment that costs $1,000 today and will provide a single return of $1,500 at the end of three years. The equation for solving the problem is $1,500 $p3/i = PV = $1,000$. The $p3/i$ factor of .667 ($1,000 ÷ $1,500) appears between 14 percent and 16 percent on the period 3 line of the "Present

Value of $1" table. The implicit interest factor of .667 is 23.5 percent (.235) of the distance between the 14 percent factor of .675 and the 16 percent factor of .641, determined as follows: .675 − .641 = .034, and .675 − .667 = .008, which, when divided by .034 = 23.5% (.235). Therefore the implicit interest rate is [(14%) + (.235) (16% − 14%)] = 14.4%.

As a second example assume that an investor wants to determine the rate of return implicit in a stock investment. The stock is selling at $60 per share and is expected to yield annual dividends of $3 at the end of each of the next five years. Also assume the investor expects to be able to sell the stock at the end of the five-year period for $80 a share. The cash flow pattern is as follows:

```
      /-------/-------/-------/-------/-------/

      0       1       2       3       4       5

    ($60)    $3      $3      $3      $3      $3
                                             $80

    PV <---------------------------------------

    PV of cash inflows = $60
```

Solution of this problem requires that the cash inflows be discounted at the rate necessary to make the present value equal the cost of the investment. This problem is similar to the equipment and lease examples except that the cash flows are not uniform in amount. It therefore becomes necessary to calculate the implicit rate on a trial-and-error basis. Normally the most efficient approach to solving such problems is to calculate the present value of the cash inflows at two rates — one that is expected to be too high and one that is expected to be too low. This results in present values that will be above and below the $60 investment cost. By interpolation a third rate can be used, which should result in a present value that equals $60. To illustrate, assume that the implicit rate is expected to be between 10 percent and 12 percent. The equations to be solved are

$$(\$3\ P5/10) + (\$80\ p5/10) = PV = [(\$3)\ (3.791)]$$
$$+ [(\$80)\ (.621)] = \$61.05.$$

$$(\$3\ P5/12) + (\$80\ p5/12) = PV = [(\$3)\ (3.605)]$$
$$+ [(\$80)\ (.567)] = \$56.18.$$

Through interpolation it is found that $60 is 78.4 percent (.784) of the distance between $56.18 and $61.05. Therefore the implicit interest rate must be 78.4 percent of the distance between 12 percent and 10 percent, or 12% − (.784) (12% − 10%) = implicit rate = 10.43%. Rates derived by interpolation are not accurate when using a wide range, such as 8 percent to 14 percent.

REFINEMENT OF PRESENT VALUE ANALYSES

The examples used to introduce present value concepts and applications assumed given cash flows, interest rates, and cash flow patterns. These variables are often not readily available in practice and must be determined using the best information available. Here we briefly discuss each element in the present and future value calculations and some factors to consider in refining the determination of each.

Determination of Initial Cash Outlays

Cash outlays included in present value analyses should include the net amount of all cash expended. The cost of stock investments, for example, should include the price of the stock, brokerage fees, and any other cash outflows directly associated with the stock acquisition.

Determination of the net amount of initial cash outlay in an equipment replacement decision involves several items. The net cash outlay calculation should reflect the delivered cost of the equipment, any cost incurred in preparing it for use, the after-tax cash received from disposal of the equipment being replaced, and the cost of any additional inventory or other working capital requirement, reduced by the present value of any subsequent reductions of that working capital.

Regardless of the types of analyses made, readers should keep in mind that the objective is to determine the net amount of cash that flows out from an individual or organization at the date of an investment or other transaction, giving effect to trade-ins, incidental expenses, various income and other taxes, and other items affecting cash.

Determination of Incremental Cash Flows

Periodic cash flows to be accumulated or discounted are often referred to as *incremental cash flows*. Like the determination of initial cash outlays, the objective in estimating periodic cash flows is to measure the net amount of additional cash inflow or outflow, taking into consideration the excess of cash receipts over cash disbursements, income taxes, and other factors affecting cash flow. The incremental effect on cash flow arising solely from the investment or other item in question — that is, the difference in cash flow with and without the investment — must be determined.

Determination of incremental cash flows normally requires estimates based on references to cash budgets, sales forecasts, suppliers' data concerning machine capacity, published records of dividends and stock prices, formal statements of cash flows published by corporations, and knowledge of economic, political, and other environmental factors, among a host of other factors. In the case of dividends, for example, the average annual percentage growth rate can be determined using present value techniques. If a company's dividends have gradually increased from $3 per share to $7 per share over a ten-year period, the growth rate can be determined by solving the equation $7 $p10/i = \$3$. The growth rate can be a significant factor in estimating likely future dividends.

An objective in estimating cash flows should be to identify factors that can significantly affect cash flows and then to refine the cash flow analysis based on analysis of those factors. One helpful technique for refining the calculation of incremental cash flows is built on the concept of expected value, which requires assigning probabilities to expected outcomes. To illustrate, assume that a management team considers all relevant factors in the decision-making process and determines that there is a 10 percent chance that incremental cash flow in an investment case will be $4,000 per year for six years. Management believes there is a 50 percent chance the amount will be $3,700, a 35 percent chance it will be $3,500, and a 5 percent chance it will be only $3,000. In completing its present value analysis, management should use an incremental cash flow figure of $3,625, determined by multiplying estimated cash flows by their respective probabilities of occurrence, as follows.

Estimated Cash Flow	Probability of Occurrence	Expected Value
$4,000	.10	$ 400
3,700	.50	1,850
3,500	.35	1,225
3,000	.05	150
Totals	1.00	$3,625

Determination of the Interest or Discount Rate

The interest rate to be used is a function of the particular present value analysis or application. In some cases, such as consumer loans, an interest rate is stated explicitly in a loan disclosure statement. Passbook savings and time certificate of deposit accounts also have set interest rates. Accountants must use incremental borrowing rates when determining the capitalizable value of leased equipment unless the lessor's implicit interest rate is less and is known. The incremental borrowing rate is an estimate of the interest rate that would be charged to a company if it were to borrow an amount sufficient to purchase (in this case) the leased asset outright, given the company's financial status and prevailing interest rates.

When the interest rate applicable to a present value analysis case is not stated or explicitly required, care should be taken to estimate a rate appropriate to the analysis. For example, equipment acquisition decisions can be made using the discounted cash flow model discussed in Chapter 4. The model uses an interest rate based on a cost of capital calculation. The underlying concept is that the asset acquired should provide a return to a company that exceeds that company's overall cost of financing. Use of an incremental borrowing rate is inappropriate because it reflects only part of a company's overall cost of financing.

In general, the rate used should reflect the risk associated with the investment or other transaction. Analysis of high-risk investments of a speculative nature therefore requires use of a discount rate well above the essentially near risk-free rates associated with savings accounts.

Inflation

Inflation poses additional difficulty in present value analyses. Adjustments for it may take the form of adjustments to incremental cash flow amounts and to interest rates used in analyses. For example, a business desiring a real rate of return of 10 percent during a period of 4 percent inflation should use a discount rate of approximately 14 percent (10% + 4%). Technically, the 14 percent rate should be increased by .4 percent (the cross-product of 10% x 4%) to adjust for the reinvestment of cash flows produced by inflation. Increasing the discount rate in this manner provides the business an inflation-adjusted or real rate of return of 10 percent.

Underlying the use of an inflation-adjusted discount rate is a requirement that cash flows also be adjusted for inflation. Presumably a constant volume of sales activity as measured in units sold will generate sales dollars that increase with inflation. The operating costs of a firm will also increase. Mathematically, if the same rate of inflation is built into the discount rate and the cash flows, the present value amounts will equal those obtained without inflation adjustments.

The rate of inflation can be determined by reference to government statistics and consideration of economic, political, and other environmental trends. One technique for measuring the rate of inflation is to compute the compound growth rate implicit in the rise of the consumer price index. In any event, inflation must be considered if present value analyses are to be meaningful, especially if the rate of inflation projected for the discount rate differs from that projected for cash flows.

2

—

Valuation

The principles of present value analysis can be used to determine the value of any cash flow through time provided an appropriate discount (interest) rate can be determined. For example, the value of investments can be determined by knowing or predicting their respective future cash flows and then discounting the cash flows to their present value using an appropriate risk rate. This chapter focuses on future cash flow determination and the critical issue of how to calculate a discount or risk rate for use in present value analyses.

VALUATION OF BONDS

The periodic cash flows (interest payments) of bonds and their maturity or terminal value are contractual: the firm or institution issuing the bond agrees to pay the investor a nominal rate or amount of interest periodically (for example, annually). At the end of the bond term, the par (principal) or maturity value is paid to the investor. Since the cash flows are known with certainty as to time and amount, a time line of future flows can be drawn. To illustrate, assume a ten-year bond with a nominal rate of 10 percent to be paid annually. The principal amount of the bond, $1,000, will be repaid at the end of the tenth year. The time line appears as follows:

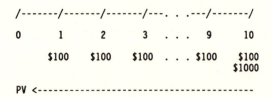

The interest payments constitute an ordinary annuity whose present value is determined using the general equation $100\ P10/10 = PV$. The par or maturity value is a single cash flow whose present value equals $1,000\ p10/10$. The complete formula is $100\ P10/10 + 1,000\ p10/10 = PV$ = issue price of the bond. Substituting the present value factors, PV = (100) (6.145) + ($1,000$) (.386) = $1,000 (rounded). (The issue price calculated is not an even $1,000 because present value interest factors contained in the tables are rounded.)

Cash flows are discounted using the market rate of interest. The preceding example assumes that the going market rate — the return investors want on their money as compensation for investment risk — is 10 percent. Because the market rate and nominal rate are the same, the selling price of the bond will equal its principal or par value of $1,000. If the market rate of interest is greater than or less than the nominal or face rate, the bond will be sold at a premium or discount — that is, an amount greater than or less than the principal or par value. For example, the interest and principal cash flows would be discounted at 8 percent if that was the market rate of interest. The present value equation would be $100\ P10/8 + 1,000\ p10/8 = PV$ = market price = (100) (6.710) + ($1,000$) (.463) = $1,134. Therefore the bond will be sold at a premium when the market rate exceeds the nominal rate of interest.

Effects of Interest Rate Changes

To see the effects of changes in interest rates on bond values, assume that the bond was purchased at the $1,000 par value and held for two years. The market rate at the end of the second year increased to 12 percent, but the firm that issued the bond continues to pay the contractual interest of 10 percent computed on par value. If the investor wants to sell at this time, the bond will have eight years to term, and the new investors will want a 12 percent return. The future cash flows will look like this to a new investor:

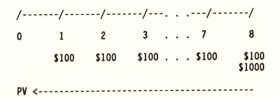

Because the discount rate or return desired by investors is now 12 percent, the selling price will be determined with this equation: ($100 P8/12) + ($1,000 p8/12) = PV. Referring to the "Present Value" tables for the appropriate factors, the equation becomes ($100) (4.968) + ($1,000) (.404) = selling price = $901 (rounded). The seller is forced to dispose of the bond at a discount because the issuing firm continues to pay only 10 percent cash interest. By offering less than the original issue price of par value, the new investor obtains a 12 percent return.

If interest rates had decreased below the 10 percent return earned by the original investor, the bond would have sold at a premium. This can be proved by calculating the value of the bond assuming the same eight years to term exist, the par value is still $1,000, and the market interest rate on this type of bond decreases to 8 percent. The present value or price should be approximately $1,115, resulting in a gain on sale by the original investor of $115 ($1,115 − $1,000).

The point of these exercises is to invest in bonds when interest rates will drop if the intent is to sell the investment before maturity. If the original investor had held the bonds to maturity, a 10 percent return would have been realized in the form of $100 annual interest plus repayment of the $1,000 investment by the issuer at maturity.

Semiannual Interest Payments

Present value factors, and hence the issue price, will change if interest payments are made in periods less than a year — for example, semiannually. Consider a $1,000 bond on which interest is paid every six months, the years to term are seven, the nominal rate is 10 percent, and the market rate of interest is 8 percent. The cash flows are illustrated in the following time line:

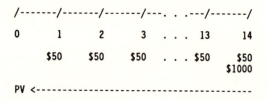

Note that the semiannual interest is $50 (half the annual interest) and is paid over fourteen periods (7 years x 2 payments per year). Again the cash flows are discounted at the market rate of interest to determine the issue price.

To get the appropriate present value factors, the 8 percent market rate must be divided by two and the number of annual time periods doubled to reflect the semiannual compounding inherent in this case. The value of the bond can then be determined with the equation $50 $P14/4$ + $1,000 $p14/4 = PV$ = market price. Substituting the appropriate present value factors, the equation becomes ($50) (10.563) + ($1,000) (.577) = $528 + $577 = $1,105. If interest payments were made quarterly, the factors would be for twenty-eight periods (7 years x 4 quarters) at a 2 percent market interest rate. Note that in all cases, both the interest and principal payments receivable under the bond investment are discounted for the same number of time periods. That is, if interest was payable quarterly, both interest and principal would be discounted twenty-eight periods to reflect quarterly compounding.

VALUATION OF CORPORATE STOCK

The valuation of stock is similar to that for bonds in that the elements used in the valuation are the same. There can be an annuity-type return on the stock in the form of quarterly or annual dividends. There is also a terminal or maturity value for the stock in terms of future selling price. Finally the risk of holding stock is taken into account by the use of a discount rate or the required return the stock investor seeks.

One of the major differences between stocks and bonds is that the cash flows on a bond are contractual while those of a stock are not. Therefore, the timing and amount of periodic dividends on stock, as well as the potential selling price (terminal value), must be predicted. Many investors argue that prediction is too difficult a task. In the business world, however, predictions are made daily about potential sales for a company, inventory requirements, and how much cash flow will be available to pay bills. Firms try to predict future stock and bond market conditions in anticipation of decisions to issue securities. And they try to predict what will happen in the money and securities markets in order to invest their short- and long-term funds.

Because predictions made in the stock market represent more risk than in the bond market, risk to the stock investor becomes greater. The greater risk assumed, and therefore the greater return desired, by the investor is accommodated by the use of a higher rate in discounting investment cash flows (returns). When the discount rate increases, the present value of cash flows decreases. Investors adjust for risk by paying a lower price for investments when there is a higher risk that cash flows will not develop as predicted.

Predicting Dividend Cash Flows

Consider potential cash flows of a stock and how one might predict them to derive a value for the stock. Remember that for stock investments, the intention is to reap the benefits of future dividends paid on the stock plus the increase in value (capital gain) obtained when the price increases over the original stock price. The investment decision is future oriented, and risks in prediction must be taken. The key is to make reasonable predictions that are neither too conservative nor too aggressive, depending on one's investment strategy or level of risk aversion.

Take a company whose dividends paid over the five years 1983–1988 increased from $3.20 to $4.28. Using present value analysis, it can be seen that this represents a 6 percent compound annual increase in dividends, determined as follows: $4.28 $p5/i = PV = 3.20. Solving the equation, the $p5/i$ factor is computed to be .748 ($3.20 ÷ $4.28). This factor is found on the period 5 line under the 6 percent column of the "Present Value of $1" table. The unknown in the equation, i, equals 6 percent, the compound annual dividend growth rate. If the $3.20 figure instead had been sales revenue in millions of dollars and five years later the company had $4.28 million in sales, the compound annual growth rate again would be 6 percent. Earnings growth can be calculated in the same manner using earnings per share data.

The growth rate calculation was shown because many times the only way to forecast the future is to look at the past and to judge whether the future will be approximately the same. Upward or downward adjustments to the growth rate can be made depending on predictions of which way future elements tend.

Referring again to the dividends, if it is decided that from 1988 to 1991 (three years) the growth rate will continue at 6 percent, the dividends can be forecast as follows:

1988	$4.28	(given)
1989	4.54	(4.28) (1.06)
1990	4.81	(4.54) (1.06)
1991	5.10	(4.81) (1.06)

Predicting Stock Selling Price or Terminal Values

An investor who wants to buy the stock in 1988 and hold it for three years has to calculate what the value of the stock will be in 1991. If experts in the market predict that the Dow Jones Index will rise from a level of 2200 points in 1988 to 2800 points in 1991, the compound growth rate of the market will be approximately 8.4 percent (2,800 $p3/i$ = 2,200, and $p3/i$ = .786), found by interpolation on the period 3 line of the "Present Value of $1" table between 8 percent and 9 percent. Using this growth rate as an estimate, the stock with a value of $80 in 1988 will increase to about $102 ($80 $a3/8.4$ = FV = $102) by 1991. Given this $102 estimated selling price or terminal value, the cash flows associated with an investment in the company's stock appear as follows (assuming the stock is acquired just after the 1988 dividend is paid):

```
    /-------/-------/-------/

    0       1       2       3

         $4.54   $4.81   $5.10
                         $102.00

    PV <---------------------
```

Selecting a Discount Rate

Since estimates of the dividend cash flows and the terminal value have been predicted, the last item that needs to be known is the *discount rate,* the rate of return the investor expects on the investment. The discount rate can be an arbitrary return the investor wants — for example, 20 percent — or it can represent an *opportunity cost,* that is, the estimated return available on alternative investments with the same risk. Even more appropriately, the discount rate may be what other investors earn on similar stock over time. Stock investors recently have been demanding approximately a 16 percent return: 10 percent to cover the pure costs of money plus inflation and 6 percent on the high side for a risk premium.

Assume that cash flows illustrated in the preceding time line are to be discounted at a 16 percent rate. The "Present Value of $1" factors must be used because the dividends are not equal in amount and hence do not constitute an annuity. The equation is $4.54 $p1/16$ + $4.81 $p2/16$ + $5.10 $p3/16$ + $102 $p3/16$ = PV = value of the stock immediately following the dividend at the end of 1988. Substituting the respective factors, the equation becomes ($4.54) (.862) + ($4.81) (.743) + ($5.10) (.641) + ($102) (.641) = $76.30, the value of the stock at the end of 1988 (Time 0 on the time line). Since the real or intrinsic value of the stock is below the 1988 market value of $80, the stock appears to be overpriced.

Not all stock cash flows should be discounted at 16 percent. This rate was used as an approximate or average figure. More sophisticated techniques, such as the capital asset pricing model and the arbitrage pricing model discussed in finance textbooks, are useful in determining risk rates for individual stocks. In general, greater risk will be associated with some stocks than with the market, and vice-versa. Discount rates derived are only approximations of the future risk of an investment. A major objective in selecting discount rates is to relate the desired return to the risk seen in the investment; as risk increases, so should the discount rate.

Additional techniques are available for calculating a stock's terminal value. In the example, the advice of experts was used to calculate the potential compound annual growth to 1991. As illustrated, the 8.4 percent compound rate was applied to the 1988 market price of $80 per share to calculate a $102 terminal value at the end of 1991. Another method some investors use to calculate the value of a stock investment requires calculation of a *capitalization rate,* an estimated yield that an investor wants on an investment. If average annual income on an investment is $1,000 and the investor wants a 10 percent return, then no more than $10,000 ($1,000 ÷ 10%) should be paid for the investment. A different way of calculating the $10,000 is to multiply the earnings of $1,000 by 10, which is the 10 percent multiple (100% ÷ 10% = 10). The multiple approach is often used in the valuation of stocks. If a stock is a very safe investment, for example, a 5 percent return might be expected, and earnings would be multiplied by 20 (100% ÷ 5%) giving a value of $20,000.

Returning to the $80 stock discussed earlier, use of the capitalization rate and earnings multiple approaches to computing terminal value can be illustrated. Assume the 1991 dividend is still projected to be $5.10 and the stock is considered an extremely safe investment. If a capitalization rate of 5 percent or an earnings multiple of twenty are considered appropriate, then the stock's projected terminal value is $102 ($5.10 x 20, or $5.10 ÷ 5%). This is the same terminal value obtained by compounding the 1988 stock price of $80 by an annual rate of 8.4 percent. Once computed, the terminal value and projected dividends would be discounted to their present value at an appropriate risk rate to determine the correct value of the stock investment.

If the stock being valued does not pay dividends, the only cash flow to be discounted is the terminal value. An estimate has to be made of the stock's potential growth in value over the planned investment period. For example, if the stock is now selling for $80, no dividends are expected, and the annual compound growth rate of the stock value is expected to be 8.4 percent over the next three years, then the terminal value would again be $102 ($80 $a3/8.4$). If the discount rate used in this case is again 16 percent, the present value of the stock would drop to $65.38. This is determined using the general equation for the present value of 1, as follows: $102 $p3/16$ = PV = ($102) (.641) = $65.38. The lower present value reflects the absence of dividends. Recall that with dividends, the present value was $76.10. In any present value calculation, dollars received in early periods are worth more than those received in later periods. Dividends eventually must be paid on the stock; however, the absence of dividends during the investor's three-year holding period affects the stock's value as indicated.

High-Growth Stock

Another example to consider is the determination of the present value of what is generally called a *high-growth stock,* one characterized by rapid growth for a period of time (for example, 40 percent compound annual rate for three years) that then tapers to a more normal growth rate (say, 6 percent). Predictions of dividends that will be paid in the first three years and the stock's terminal value at the end of three years must take into account the lower growth potential after Year 3.

The first step in this case is to calculate the 40 percent compound growth in dividends. Starting with the $4.28 annual dividend paid at the end of 1988 in the original stock example, the dividends for the next three years can be forecast as follows:

1988	$4.28	(given)
1989	5.99	(4.28) (1.40)
1990	8.39	(5.99) (1.40)
1991	11.74	(8.39) (1.40)

Next, the terminal value of the stock must be calculated, taking into account the reduced growth of the stock. One way to do this is to take a common finance formula that incorporates the growth of the stock and the rate of return investors require. Most basic finance principles books show the derivation and proof for the formula: $TV = D \div (R - G)$, where

TV is the terminal value of the stock,
D is the last dividend in the holding period multiplied by 1 plus the growth rate,
R is the rate of return required by the investor, and
G is the growth rate.

Substituting the appropriate numbers into the formula: $TV = (\$11.74)$ $(1.06) \div (16\% - 6\%) = \$12.44 \div .10 = \$124.40$. The last dividend at the end of the three-year holding period was $11.74, and 6 percent is the growth rate expected after Year 3. Sixteen percent was used as the rate of return desired by the investor because it represents an average return for a stock in this risk class.

The following time line illustrates the dividend cash flow and the terminal value of the stock for the 1989–1991 (three-year holding period):

```
        /-------/-------/-------/

    0       1       2       3

          $5.99   $8.39   $11.74
                          $124.40

    PV <----------------------
```

The value of the stock at time zero (the beginning of 1989, after the 1988 end-of-year dividend) can now be calculated by discounting the future cash flows at the required 16 percent rate of return. The Year 3 dividend and terminal value (expected selling price) can be discounted together because both cash flows occur at the same time. The present value formula is $\$5.99\ p1/16 + \$8.39\ p2/16 + \$136.14\ p3/16 = PV$. Substituting appropriate factors from the "Present Value of $1" table, the equation becomes ($5.99) (.862) + ($8.39) (.743) + ($136.14) (.641) = PV = $98.65 = the value of the stock. Note that the value of the high-growth stock is necessarily higher than that of the moderate-growth stock illustrated earlier because of the higher dividends and the higher terminal value that the stock should command in the market.

Present value analysis has been used to calculate growth rates and to discount future cash flows. All future dollars were standardized to today's dollars. Only when dollars have been standardized in terms of present value can any meaningful comparisons be made among investments. Because cash flows may vary by timing and by dollar amount, the only way to know their comparative worth is through the use of present value analysis. Of all the techniques used in finance, time value of money is the most important.

VALUATION OF FIRMS

When an investor places money in an investment, the expectation is that the future cash flows will exceed the amount invested. Note that the important element here is *future* cash flows. An investor buys stock based on expectations of future dividends and terminal value. If an art investor buys a painting, the hope is that the painting will increase in value or, stated in financial terms, that the terminal value of the art will exceed its cost. Similarly when an investor buys a firm, the expectation is that future cash flows will reward the investor with a return appropriate for the level of risk assumed.

The only reason for an investor to buy a stock, a work of art, or a viable firm and not have the expectation of an appropriate level of future cash flows would be if the investments were made to generate psychic rewards instead of income. The holder of a blue chip stock could brag about owning it, the buyer of the Renoir would derive satisfaction from being considered an art connoisseur, and the purchaser of a firm could say with pride that he was his own boss.

We stress these points because some valuation methods use past income rather than future cash flows to calculate value. Only expected future cash flows are relevant in making investment decisions, however. Past income and cash flows are accomplished and cannot be changed or recovered. Unfortunately, past income has been used by some individuals in accounting and finance, and even courts of law have relied heavily on past income for determining the value of a business.

While past income and cash flows are certain and their related trend lines can be calculated, growth rates and discount rates must be applied to future potential cash flows. The example presented compares the value of a firm using past cash flows with the present value of future flows. A determination can then be made of which method is more appropriate for use in a valuation decision.

Assume a firm, F-Co., has the financial history presented in Table 2.1. The pertinent years to be evaluated plus earnings and cash flows of F-Co. are listed. Because only earnings and cash flows are important in this example, entire balance sheets and income statements are not shown. Note that only three years of earnings and cash flows are projected. Beyond that time period, the accuracy of amounts becomes questionable. Terminal value calculations at the end of the third year can be used to value earnings and cash flows in the fourth and following years.

Only after-tax cash flows should be considered. Cash flows are defined as earnings after taxes plus noncash operating charges (expenses), such as depreciation. Depreciation and other noncash charges, unlike salaries and other operating expenses, do not require cash outflows and are therefore added back to earnings in computing after-tax cash flows available to provide investors a return on investment plus recovery of the amounts invested.

Capitalization of Earnings Valuation

The first valuation of F-Co. will be completed using only past earnings, not cash flows. This will result in two serious errors: (1) only historical or past earnings will be considered, and (2) after-tax cash flows will be ignored. This valuation approach, called the *capitalization of earnings method,* is one of the methods favored by the Internal Revenue Service and therefore is widely accepted. The method affords the surety

TABLE 2.1
Selected Financial Data of F-Co.

Year	Earnings in Thousands	Cash Flows
X-3	$ 159.2	$ 265.3
X-2	183.6	291.1
X-1	209.3	308.7
X+1	207.1	323.2
X+2	218.4	342.5
X+3	231.2	362.1

of past numbers and simplifies calculations. Past earnings are weighted, with the most recent earnings given greater weight. A weighted average earnings amount is then obtained. Finally, a capitalization rate (or a multiple, as discussed in the section on stock valuation) can be applied to determine the value of the firm.

The steps followed under the capitalization of earnings method are reflected in schedule (2.1). First, historical earnings after taxes are listed. Second, the earnings are weighted giving greatest weight to the most recent earnings. In this case a weight of 3 was assigned to the most recent (X–1) earnings. The next step is to multiply the appropriate earnings by the weights indicated. For example, the X–1 earnings of $209.3 (thous-ands) is multiplied by 3 to get weighted earnings of $627.9. The weight-ed earnings are then added together to derive the total weighted income of $1,154.3. Next, the weights are added together and then divided into the total weighted earnings to get the weighted average earnings of $192.4. In the final step, weighted average earnings are divided by a discount rate appropriate to this kind of risk. In this case $192.4 is divided by 20 percent to arrive at a value for F-Co. of $962, or $962,000. Note that a discount rate higher than 16 percent was used since it was assumed that F-Co. is a private company not listed on any stock exchange. Some might argue for use of an even higher discount rate to reflect risk.

Under the capitalization of earnings method, no use was made of present value calculations. The dollars of period X–3 were valued the same as X–1 dollars. Also no attempt was made to project potential

(2.1)	After Tax Earnings	Assigned Weight	Weighted Earnings
Year X-3	$159.2	1	$159.2
Year X-2	183.6	2	367.2
Year X-1	209.3	3	627.9
Total weighted earnings			$1,154.3
Total weights (1+2+3)			6
Weighted average earnings ($1,154.3/6)			192.4
Capitalization rate			.20
F-Co value			$962.0

earnings that a buyer of F-Co. might obtain from operating the firm. A new owner of F-Co. should be more concerned with future earnings since that is what will provide the cash flow for recouping the investment, as well as a return for the risk taken.

Discounted Earnings Valuation

Under the second valuation method to be considered, not only will the earnings of F-Co. be projected into the future (see the earlier illustration for X+1, X+2, and X+3 earnings), but a present value of the firm will be calculated. Note that in this example, the future earnings of F-Co. are used, not the future cash flows. A later example will demonstrate discounting of after-tax cash flows to arrive at a valuation of F-Co. Future earnings are discounted in the present case so a comparison can be made between values calculated using past earnings (capitalization of earnings) versus future earnings (discounted future earnings).

Future earnings of F-Co. were estimated by considering the past and then adjusting for likely future circumstances. Past earnings can be used to estimate the potential growth rate of future earnings. (The technique of using present value tables to calculate growth rates was used in the stock valuation section.) Past earnings grew from $159,200 in X–3 to $209,300 in X–1, a compound annual growth rate of 14.6 percent, calculated as follows: $209,300 $p2/i = PV$ = $159,200. Solving the equation, the $p2/i$ factor is .761, found between 14 and 16 percent on the period 2 line of the "Present Value of $1" table. The 14.6 percent rate was determined by interpolation. The $p2/i$ factor of .761 is 30.8 percent of the distance between the 14 and 16 percent factors of .769 and .743, respectively. Two percent times 30.8 percent is about .6 percent, which when added to 14 percent equals 14.6 percent.

If F-Co. earnings are expected to follow their historical trend, a starting growth rate to consider for future earnings is 14.6 percent. However, F-Co. was looking at a potential economic downturn as well as an industry downturn. For this reason, it was estimated that the same or slightly lower earnings would result for X+1. Because of the strength of the firm, only a slight decrease would result, and for this reason earnings were estimated to be $207.1 (in thousands). Increases of 5.5 percent and 5.9 percent annual rate were forecast for years X+2 and X+3, respectively. Earnings therefore are as follows:

X+1	207.1	(given)
X+2	218.5	(207.1) (105.5)
X+3	231.4	(218.5) (105.9)

To complete the F-Co. valuation, it is necessary to compute the terminal value at the end of the third period (X+3) and the appropriate discount rate. The discount rate can be the same as the capitalization rate used previously for F-Co. — 20 percent. The risk rate of the firm may have increased slightly because earnings have leveled off; however, for purposes of this example, 20 percent will be used.

The terminal value can be calculated by using the terminal value formula used earlier in the high-growth stock valuation example. The formula requires the substitution of earnings (E) for dividends (D) for a business valuation, as follows: $TV = E \div (R - G)$, where

TV · is the terminal value of the business,
E is after-tax earnings projected for X+3 multiplied by 1 plus the growth rate,
R is the rate of return required by the investor, and
G is the growth rate.

Inserting the appropriate numbers, the equation becomes: $TV = (\$231.4)$ $(1 + .04) \div (.20 - .04) = \$1,504.1$.

Recall that the long-term growth rate for this firm beyond the X+3 period was estimated to be 4 percent and that 20 percent (.20) was identified as the discount rate. The following time line reflects the earnings and terminal value estimates for the three years following acquisition of the company:

```
/----------/----------/----------/
0       X+1        X+2        X+3

        $207.1     $218.5     $231.4
                              $1,504.1

PV <-------------------------------
```

The amounts indicated can now be discounted to their present value using the 20 percent rate of return required by the investor. The equation is ($207.1 $p1/20$) + ($218.5 $p2/20$) + ($231.4 $p3/20$) + ($1.504.1 $p3/20$) = PV = value of F-Co. Combining the year X+3 amounts of $231.4 and $1.504.1 and then substituting the present value factors, the equation becomes ($207.1) (.833) + ($218.54) (.694) + ($1735.5) (.579) = $1.329.0 (or $1,329,000). Observe that under the discounted future earnings method, the value of the firm is calculated to be $367,000 greater ($1,329,000 − $962,000) than the value obtained capitalizing historical earnings. It is interesting to note that the net worth of F-Co. at the end of period X−1 was $1,674,400 (based on facts not listed in the book).

Discounted Cash Flow Valuation

The correct way to value a firm is to discount future after-tax cash flows at an appropriate discount rate. This method of valuation will now be illustrated. Referring to Table 2.1, the after-tax cash flows are found to be $323.2 (thousands) in year X+1, $342.5 in X+2, and $362.1 in X+3. The cash flows projected are based on assumed growth rates of 4.7 percent, 6.9 percent, and 5.7 percent, respectively, for the three years. Recall that although earnings dropped slightly in the first year, calculated cash flows increased 4.6 percent after noncash charges were added back to earnings. When calculating terminal value, it will again be estimated that the long-run growth rate of the firm after Year 3 (X+3) will be 4 percent. All cash flows will be discounted at 20 percent, the rate of return the investor requires for the risk associated with the investment in F-Co.

The terminal value calculation again requires use of the general terminal valuation formula. In this case it is modified to read as follows: $TV = CF \div (R - G)$, where

TV is the terminal value of the investment in F-Co.,
CF is the cash flow projected for year X+3 multiplied by 1 plus the growth rate,
R is the rate of return required by the investor, and
G is the growth rate.

Substituting the appropriate numbers into the equation, $TV = [(362.1) (1 + .04)] \div (.20 - .04) = $2,353.6$ (or $2,353,600). Future cash flows projected for the investment in F-Co. are summarized in the following time line:

```
/----------/----------/----------/
0        X+1        X+2        X+3

         $323.2     $342.5     $362.1
                               $2,353.6

PV <---------------------------------
```

The cash flows illustrated can now be discounted using factors from the "Present Value of $1" table for periods of one, two, and three years, as follows: ($323.2) (.833) + ($342.5) (.694) + ($2,715.9) (.579) = PV = $2,079.2 ($2,079,200) = value of F-Co.

In this example, the present value of F-Co. cash flows was higher than its net worth ($1,674,400). This will not always be the case. The value also depends on the type of industry the firm is in and how efficiently the firm is using its assets to generate earnings. An ideal kind of firm to buy is one that is too heavy in assets and has significant amounts of unnecessary expenses in the income statement (it thus has a low value and, hence, investment cost). The firm will be generating minimum earnings and, consequently, poor cash flows. In this case, it may be possible that the net worth (or book value) of the firm is higher than the present value of future cash flows. The investor could reduce assets to more reasonable levels, reduce expenses, and perhaps apply a leveraged buy-out to make good profits. The key is knowing the nature of the turnaround to be effected.

Present value analysis is important not only in the valuation of market instruments such as stocks and bonds but also in valuing any cash flow stream. Investors should determine the future cash flow potential of investments. Since the timing and amounts of investment cash flows vary, it is important that they be standardized by the calculation of present values; that is, all dollars should be stated in terms of today's dollars.

3

Investment Decision Rules

Many important questions are raised when a firm or individual is determining whether to buy new equipment, sell old equipment, or a combination of both. The same questions exist when a firm is analyzing a new product or wants to expand into a new sales area. These are all investment-type decisions that involve past and future cash flows.

Investment decisions require a decision rule or ranking method. Judgments have to be made about which cash flows are relevant and should be included in analyses. A response must be made to the question of risk. Appropriate depreciation methods must also be considered. Finally, the ability to make reasonable cash flow projections becomes critical.

The first question to be considered is that of decision rules. Investors and firms use a variety of analytical methods, ranging from the simple to the complex, to determine what investments should be made. This chapter reviews some of the more popular methods and includes discussion of the major advantages and disadvantages of each. There is no perfect method or decision rule. The theoretically best method may be difficult to implement, thereby making a less sophisticated method more useful for a given decision.

Among the methods used to make investment decisions are payback, accounting return on investment, net present value, and internal rate of return. Only the latter two methods require use of present value analysis. These four methods will be illustrated using a simple set of decision variables. Depending on the methods used, very different decision responses may result. The payback method produces an answer in time. The accounting return on investment and internal rate of return methods result in percentage responses. And the net present value method provides an answer in dollars.

PAYBACK METHOD

The payback method is used to determine how rapidly cash flows return an amount that has been invested. After-tax cash flows for various investments presented in Table 3.1 are used to illustrate application of the payback method. Investment L requires an investment of $2,400, and investments M and G each require a $2,000 investment. All investments are assumed to be made at the beginning of time period zero; therefore the present value of each investment is simply the amount invested.

Assume there is sufficient money to make only one investment. The amount invested in L will be returned in 2.4 years ($2,400 ÷ $1,000). The payback periods for investments M and G are the same — two years — although M receives $500 the first year and $1,500 the second year, while G receives nothing the first year and $2,000 the second year.

Several shortcomings of the payback method become apparent. Because the investment with the shortest payback is considered the most desirable, investments M and G would be selected over L although $3,000 of cash flow would result for L compared to $2,500 for M and $2,400 for G. Thus the payback system does not take into account cash flows beyond the payback period.

Another weakness of the method is that investments may be rated the same although their cash flow patterns differ. In the illustration, note that M and G are rated the same; however, if the time value of money is considered, investment M is better (as shown later in this chapter). The payback system ignores the timing and amount of cash flows. Only absolute dollar amounts are considered, not the timing and present value of individual sums. The payback method will not differentiate in the

TABLE 3.1
After-tax Cash Flows of Investment Alternatives

Year	Investment L	Investment M	Investment G
0	$(2,400)	$(2,000)	$(2,000)
1	1,000	500	0
2	1,000	1,500	2,000
3	1,000	500	400

circumstances given which investment is best. Only one investment can be made, but M and G are considered equal.

A third weakness of payback is that only the recovery of principal is considered; the percentage return on cash investment is not determined. Presumably investors will not invest unless there is an appropriate return. Since return on investment is not calculated under the payback method, the investor must determine whether there is a return and, if so, of what rate.

In summary, the payback method is not good for evaluating investments, but many investors continue to use it. An advantage of the method seems to be that investors are forced to pick investments with the earliest liquidity. Considering the time value of money, this type of choice might be preferable; however, the shortcomings of the payback method are serious and may result in incorrect choices. Therefore the method should rarely be used by itself.

ACCOUNTING RETURN ON INVESTMENT

Under the accounting return on investment (accounting ROI) method, the investment with the highest return is selected. The return is determined by dividing average annual income on an investment by the average investment. For example, assume that the after-tax cash flows of Table 3.1 are instead net income figures and that the salvage value (ending value) of each investment is zero. These numbers can be used to calculate accounting ROI.

For investment G, the average annual income is ($2,000 + $400) ÷ 3 years, or $800. The average investment is $1,000 ($2,000 beginning investment + ending salvage value of 0) ÷ 2. The accounting ROI for G equals $800 ÷ $1,000, or 80 percent. The accounting ROI for both L and M is 83.33 percent, calculated in the same manner. Given these returns, L and M would be considered preferable to investment G. Note that under the accounting ROI method of evaluating investment, L and M are considered equal, while G is the least desirable. Under the payback method, M and G were equal, while L was the least desirable.

A major flaw of the accounting ROI method is that all dollars are treated equally. Like the payback method, the time value of money is not taken into account. Early investment returns are treated as equal to later returns. Another problem is that the order in which earnings occur is not taken into account. As can be seen in Table 3.1 (assuming again that cash flows are treated as net income figures), both M and G receive $2,000 of inflows in the first two years, while M gets $500 the first year and $1,500 the second year. Investment G returns nothing the first year and $2,000 the second year. All these dollars are treated as being of equal value although early dollars can be reinvested to generate more returns.

NET PRESENT VALUE METHOD

Under the net present value (NPV) method, the investment with the highest NPV should be selected when investments are mutually exclusive. In other cases, a performance or profitability index is used to rank investments. NPV is the difference between the present value of cash inflows and present value of cash outflows for each investment. The formulas to be used are applied to investments L, M, and G. The amounts in Table 3.1, including for the investments in time period zero, will be considered after-tax cash flows. The discount rate used to calculate present values is assumed to be 10 percent.

The equation for calculating the NPV of investment L follows: ($1,000 $P3/10$) − $2,400, where $1,000 is the annual investment return, $P3/10$ is the present value factor for a three-period annuity, and $2,400 is the net cash outlay or net investment cost. Substituting the appropriate present value factor, NPV of L = ($1,000) (2.487) − $2,400 = $2,487 − $2,400 = $87 = the excess of the present value of future cash flows over the net investment.

For investment M, the equation is NPV of M = [($500 $p1/10$) + ($1,500 $p2/10$) + ($500 $p3/10$)] − $2,000 net cash outlay. Inserting the correct present value factors, NPV of M = [($500) (.909)] + [($1,500) (.826)] + [($500) (.751)] − $2,000 = $454 + $1,239 + $376 − $2,000 = $69. Following the same approach, the NPV of investment G is calculated to be −$48.

The NPV computations show that L is the best investment because it has the highest NPV ($87 compared to $69 for M and −$48 for G). However, the three alternatives do not require equal investments. If the investments are mutually exclusive, L should be accepted because it increases the wealth of the firm by the greatest amount. When alternatives require unequal investments but are not mutually exclusive, a performance or profitability index has to be calculated. The performance index relates the present value cash inflows to the present value cash outflows. For investment L, for example, the calculation would be $2,487 (present value of cash inflows) ÷ $2,400 (present value of cash outflows), which equals 1.0363. A summary of the performance indexes is shown in (3.1).

If only investments M and G are being compared, the higher NPV could be used to distinguish the better alternative because the investment in each project is $2,000; however, the performance indexes have to be used to distinguish among the three alternatives. The index for L is the highest, and next is M. Investment G is the least desirable. In fact, it should be rejected since it has a negative NPV. Only projects with a positive NPV or positive performance index will increase the wealth of the investor.

Advantages of the NPV method of evaluating investments are that it takes into account the time value of money, considers returns beyond the payback period, incorporates some return on investments to accommodate the risk element, considers the timing and amount of each cash flow, and provides evaluations based on dollars and a performance index.

The major disadvantage of the method is that the real or intrinsic risk of investments is sometimes unknown. Therefore a proxy discount rate (here 10 percent was used) must be applied in analyses. The discount rate may be a judgment of what the investor thinks the risk of the cash flow is.

Another limitation of NPV is that the discount rate used is the implied return that will presumably be earned on all cash inflows. For example, referring to Table 3.1, investment M has an inflow of $500 in the first year. The presumption is that the $500 inflow can be reinvested to generate a return of 10 percent (the discount rate used in the NPV calculation of M). And the $1,500 inflow in Year 2 is presumed to be reinvested at the 10 percent rate. If reinvestment at the discount rate is not possible on all the cash inflows of M, then the investment cannot meet the implied assumptions, and the NPV calculation is not valid. Therefore, a condition of the NPV method is that the reinvestment rate must be attainable for calculations to be valid. If not, then a lower discount rate should be used.

(3.1)

Investment	PV of Cash Inflow	PV of Cash Outflow	Performance Index
L	$2,487	$2,400	1.0363
M	2,069	2,000	1.0345
G	1,952	2,000	.9762

INTERNAL RATE OF RETURN METHOD

Internal rate of return (IRR) is defined as the discount rate that equates the present value of cash inflows with the present value of cash outflows. Stated differently, the IRR is that discount rate which makes the present value of cash inflows equal the present value of cash outflows (normally the dollar amount invested) so that the difference is zero. For example, using the cash flows for investment M (see Table 3.1), the question to be answered is what discount rate will make the cash inflows of $500, $1,500, and $500 in Years 1, 2, and 3, respectively, have a present value of $2,000 (the present value of the outflows). If the present value of the cash inflows ($2,000) equals the present value of the cash outflows ($2,000), the difference will be zero.

When M's cash inflows were discounted at 10 percent in a previous example, the present value was $2,069. Because the investment cash outflow was $2,000, the difference was a positive NPV of $69. The internal rate of return for M then must be higher than 10 percent because the NPV was greater than zero. To reduce the $69 NPV to zero will require that the cash inflows be discounted at some rate greater than 10 percent. (Remember that as the discount rate increases, the present value decreases. A corollary is that the greater the risk of an investment, the lower the price to be paid for that investment.) The question then becomes what rate higher than 10 percent should be used to equate the present value of the cash inflows with the outflows. In other words, how much greater than 10 percent must the discount rate be to get a difference of zero?

There are several ways to determine the internal rate of return. The easiest is to use a computer or financial calculator. Without such assistance, the IRR can be determined using present value equations. For investments with equal periodic cash inflows such as investment L, the calculation is straightforward; however, when cash inflows are uneven, as for investments M and G, a trial-and-error method must be used to determine the IRR.

Even Cash Flows

To determine the IRR of L (even cash flows), use the equation for the present value of an ordinary annuity, as follows: $1,000 $P3/i = PV = $2,400$, where $1,000 represents the annual investment cash flows, $P3/i$ is the three-period factor for an unknown interest rate, and $2,400 is the cost of the investment. Solving the equation, the factor is determined to be 2.400 (investment ÷ cash inflows). Referring to the period 3 line in the "Present Value of an Ordinary Annuity of $1" table, the 2.400 factor is found to lie between the 12 percent and 14 percent factors of 2.404 and 2.322, respectively. By interpolation, the 2.400 factor is determined to be .002 (2.402 − 2.400) of the .080 (2.402 − 2.322) distance between the two interest factors. Therefore, the IRR equals .12 + (.02) (.002 ÷ .080) = .1205, or 12.05 percent. The fraction .002 divided by .080 is multiplied by .02 because .02 is the difference between 12 and 14 percent.

The IRR calculations for M and G are more difficult because the cash inflows are uneven. Therefore a trial-and-error method must be used. The cash flows must be discounted at different rates until the present value of cash inflows equals the present value of cash outflows. In this case, the investment cash outflow occurs at time period zero and does not need to be discounted. As determined earlier, the cash inflows of investment M discounted at 10 percent yielded a positive NPV of $69. Therefore the IRR has to be greater than 10 percent.

If a 12 percent discount rate is used as an estimate, the present value of the cash inflows equals ($500 $p1/i$) + ($1,500 $p2/i$) + ($500 $p3/i$). Substituting the "Present Value of $1" factors of .892, .797, and .712 for Years 1, 2, and 3, respectively, the present value is calculated to be $1,998, just $2 less than the $2,000 cost of investment M. Therefore the IRR is about 12 percent. To get a more accurate IRR figure, it will be necessary to interpolate. The present value calculated by discounting at the IRR is $69 ($2,069 − $2,000) of the $71 ($2,069 − $1,998) distance between 10 and 12 percent. The IRR calculation becomes .10 + (.02) (69 ÷ 71) = .1194, or 11.94 percent. Again the .02 in the final calculation represents the difference between 10 and 12 percent (.12 − .10) where the estimated IRR is located.

The process used for investment M must be used to calculate the IRR of G. Since the 10 percent rate used in the earlier NPV analysis resulted in a negative NPV — that is, a present value less than $2,000 — the IRR has to be less than 10 percent. Estimating that 8 percent is too low an estimate of the IRR, the present value is calculated to be $2,032. Since the present value at 8 percent exceeds $2,000, the IRR must be between 8 and 10 percent. By interpolation the IRR is calculated to be 8.8 percent.

Note when interpolating to determine IRR that the range should be no more than about 2 percent. The nature of the mathematical progression of percentage value factors will cause interpolation between distant percentages — for example, 8 percent and 14 percent — to be in error. A question may arise as to why the NPV of G computed using 10 percent is negative although the investment provides a return of positive 8.8 percent. The answer is that the IRR of G will always be 8.8 percent, regardless of the discount rate used to determine the NPV of the investment. There is only one IRR for investment G, but there can be several different NPV amounts depending on the discount rate used. For example, the NPV of G using a 10 percent discount rate was –$48, compared to +$32 using an 8 percent discount rate. The IRR is a measure of the effective yield on an investment, that is, the compound annual interest difference between the investment cash outflows and cash inflows. The NPV method, on the other hand, assumes that some target investment return, the discount rate, is desirable and therefore discounts the cash flows by that desired rate. Investments with an IRR greater than the acceptable discount rate will have a positive NPV. In the case of investment G, the NPV will be positive up to an 8.8 percent discount rate. However, when cash flows are discounted at a target or desired return greater than 8.8 percent, the NPV of G will become negative.

The following summary of IRRs for the three investments illustrated that investment L has the highest IRR. Therefore it is the most desirable investment.

Investment	IRR
L	12.05%
M	11.94%
G	8.8 %

Evaluation of the IRR Method

One of the major advantages of using the IRR method for evaluating investments is that the compound interest rate of return implicit in an investment is calculated. Other advantages are that the time value of money is considered, cash inflows beyond the payback period are recognized, and results can be compared to cost of capital percentages. The major disadvantage is that in unique circumstances, there can be several rates of return for the same investment. This can occur when there are several sign changes in the cash flows from positive to negative, and vice-versa. The usual investment involves only one sign change — that from the negative investment to the positive cash inflows, as in investments L, M, and G. The topic of multiple IRRs for the same investment is an advanced topic that is not discussed further in this book.

Another shortcoming of the IRR method lies with the implicit reinvestment rate. Recall that under the NPV method, all cash inflows are presumed to be reinvested at the discount rate. And under the IRR method, the presumption is that all cash inflows can be reinvested at the IRR. This can lead to rejection of an investment with a one-time-high IRR and cash flows that cannot be reinvested at that high rate. Adjusted IRRs, an advanced topic not covered in this book, are used to overcome this reinvestment problem.

A final flaw in the IRR method is that it does not evaluate the real or intrinsic risk of an investment. The IRR may be 15 percent, but the real risk of the investment may be much higher, for example, 25 percent. A judgment must necessarily be made whether the IRR compensates for the risks being assumed. In Chapter 2, it was noted that for other than contractual-type investments like bonds, it is difficult to know what an investment's intrinsic risk is, and for that reason a proxy rate is used.

EVALUATION OF RANKING METHODS

Schedule (3.2) summarizes the rankings of investments L, M, and G according to the four ranking methods illustrated. Only the NPV and IRR methods provide consistent evaluations and can distinguish among the three investments. Under three methods, investment G was identified as the worst, but under the payback method, it was tied for best. The accounting ROI method did not distinguish between L and M and therefore identifies them as tied for best investment. Given the preceding facts and other reasons cited earlier, NPV and IRR are the best ranking methods and are usually consistent with each other. Because the IRR method may produce multiple rates of return in some instances, the NPV is the safest ranking method to use. Further, the NPV method provides the best solution for decisions involving multiple investments and a limited amount of investment capital. However, the IRR method will be illustrated for capital budgeting decisions when a comparison with cost of capital is necessary and no multiple sign changes occur to cause multiple IRRs.

(3.2)

Ranking Method	Best Investments	Intermediate Investment	Worst Investment
Payback	M, G (tie)	-	L
Accounting ROI	L, M (tie)	-	G
NPV	L	M	G
IRR	L	M	G

DEVELOPING DISCOUNT RATES

Assumed discount rates are used in many examples throughout this book. In practice, investors must select discount rates that reflect the true or intrinsic risk of investments, a desired rate of return, or, at a minimum, the cost of capital. Ideally investors should make evaluations based on the intrinsic risk of investments. Because intrinsic risk is difficult to determine, a desired rate of return or cost of capital rate is used as a proxy.

A number of methods can be used to determine the desired rate of return or cost of capital. Only the most popularly used methods will be discussed in this chapter. Some methods apply only to stocks, others to bonds, and others to general investments (for example, in companies and equipment).

Price-Earnings Multiple

The most common method for determining a discount rate for cash flows on stocks is the price-earnings (P/E) multiple. Assume that a given industry's earnings have historically been capitalized at 10 percent; that is, the industry P/E multiple has been ten times earnings (100% ÷ 10% = 10 times). The price of a company's stock in that industry will be determined by multiplying the next year's forecasted earnings by the industry multiple. Historical capitalization rates are usually determined by research for specific industries and adjusted for potential future conditions before being applied to future earnings. One of the major weaknesses of using P/E multiples is that they assume an investor will receive the earnings of the business. The P/E multiple may be useful in predicting earnings of a business but not for predicting investment cash flows. It is important to remember that the cash flows arising from an investment in a public company are the dividends paid, not the earnings reported, and the capital gain or loss realized for the difference between the price paid and the price received when the stock investment is sold.

Dividend Formula

Another technique for calculating a discount rate or required investment return on stocks is to use a dividend equation or formula. The formula bases stock investment returns on dividend yields and growth rates. The formula is $R = (D \div P) + g$, where

R is the return on the stock,
D is the next expected dividend,
P is the current price of the stock, and
g is the expected dividend growth rate.

For example, if the current price of a stock is $30 and the next expected annual dividend is $3.00, then $D \div P = \$3 \div \$30 = 10\%$. Therefore, the dividend yield portion of the formula requires a 10 percent return. If dividends are expected to grow at an annual rate of 6 percent, then $R = 10\% + 6\% = 16\%$, the rate at which to discount cash flows on the stock investment.

Capital Asset Pricing Model

A final way of determining a desired yield or discount rate on stock is to use the capital asset pricing model (CAPM), which contains two elements: (1) the risk-free rate or pure cost of money plus an adjustment (allowance) for inflation and (2) the risk premium on a given investment. The model formula is $CAPM = RF + B(RM - RF)$, where

$CAPM$ is the capital asset pricing model discount rate,
  RF is the risk-free rate or pure cost of money plus an allowance for inflation,
   B is the beta of the stock or investment, and
  RM is the market risk.

The risk-free rate (RF) can be measured at the current yield on one-year treasury bills if the investment is short term. Yields on five- to ten-year treasury notes or bonds can be used for long-term investments. Assume an investment is to be held for about five years and that the average yield on five-year treasury notes is 8.6 percent. (Historical averages of these rates are sometimes used.) The next element in the model is B (beta), which represents the volatility of the stock in the market. For example, assume that when the stock market goes up 10 percent (increase in the Dow-Jones average, for example), the market price of the proposed stock investment consistently rises 10 percent. The beta of the stock will be 1 (10% ÷ 10%). Betas on stocks calculated by several services, including Value Line, can be used for CAPM purposes. Note that betas can and do change; therefore it is important that current betas be used.

To continue the example, assume that the stock's beta is 1. The market risk (RM) is normally composed of the risk-free rate ($RF = 8.6\%$) plus a risk premium for stocks in general. Risk premiums might range from 3 to 6 percent. Adding a risk premium rate of 6 percent to the 8.6 percent risk-free rate, RM becomes 14.6 percent. Substituting the appropriate numbers the CAPM formula becomes $CAPM = 8.6\% + 1(14.6\% - 8.6\%) = 14.6$ percent. The rate of 14.6 percent reflects the risk associated with the stock and should be used to discount the projected investment cash flows. If the beta on the stock had been 1.2, the discount rate would have been 15.8 percent, calculated as follows: $CAPM = RF + B(MR - RF) = 8.6\% + (1.2) (14.6\% - 8.6\%) = 8.6\% + 7.2\% = 15.8\%$. The risk-free element of the formula is measured at 8.6 percent, with the risk premium of 7.2 percent added to reflect total risk of the stock at 15.8 percent.

A problem with using CAPM is that the elements of the formula should be based on forecasted estimates of RF, B, and MR. Since forecasting these elements is a difficult task, historical numbers or estimates adjusted for judgments about future potential are used. Another problem is that CAPM is a static (one-point-in-time) model. Given that the market is constantly changing, a dynamic model should be used. One dynamic model, the arbitrage pricing theory, is being tested and at some future date may be used, possibly in a modified form. Until then, the CAPM model can be used, provided its limitations are considered. Where portfolios of stocks are being developed, more complex adjustments must be taken into account. Refer to an investment theory textbook for more information on this subject.

Other Discount Rate Techniques

Discount rates to be used on bond cash flows should reflect the current market rate required to issue bonds of a certain category. For example, assume a bond issued three years ago has a nominal and yield rate (rate at which issued) of 9 percent. To be issued in the current market, the bond would have to yield 10 percent, the current market rate. That is, remaining cost flows on the bond would have to be discounted at 10 percent to determine the current market value of the bond. The discount rate should be based on research of the rates that similar bonds are yielding in the current market. The going market rate reflects the risk or required return investors desire.

The calculation of discount rates to be used for general investments is very difficult. What return should be required for a new uranium mining venture or for a new auto engine design? The risk of these investments will necessarily be higher than for more usual investments. Because of the difficulty of measuring the risk of general investments, investors begin by calculating their cost of capital. For example, if equity financing for a project can be obtained at a rate higher than for actively traded stocks, say 20 percent, that equity cost must be factored with the cost of other funds borrowed for the project. The final rate depends on the mix of debt and equity used to finance the uranium mine or engine design projects.

To illustrate, assume that project E will have a mix of 60 percent equity financing at a 20 percent rate and 40 percent debt financing at a cost of 14 percent. The weighted average cost of capital is calculated as follows:

Equity financing = (.60) (.20) = .12, or 12.0 percent
Debt financing =   (.40) (.14) = .056, or 5.6 percent
Weighted average cost of capital =   17.6 percent

Thus, 17.6 percent is an approximate minimum cost of capital financing that must be covered by the project investment. In order for this project to generate the exact return desired, the cash inflows (earnings after taxes plus depreciation) must be large enough so that when discounted at 17.6 percent, the NPV will equal zero; that is, the IRR will equal 17.6 percent. If the NPV is greater than zero, the return to investors will exceed the weighted average cost of capital (financing). In fact, equity investors will earn more than 20 percent because any excess returns accrue to the equity holders. The contractual agreement with creditors provides them a fixed return of 14 percent.

The next question to be answered is whether the true (intrinsic) risk on project E is 17.6 percent. Although the rate is the weighted average cost of debt and equity financing charged by investors, it likely has no correlation to the intrinsic risk of the investment. The actual risk may be much higher than the 17.6 percent weighted average return required by investors. Since there is no known way to identify an intrinsic or true risk rate, the return an investor wants must be based on judgment, especially if there is no prior experience.

One way of deciding required return is to consider other investment opportunities. An attempt can be made to obtain returns that exceed the best of other alternatives investors might have. This is called an *opportunity cost approach* to discount rates. An evaluation can be made of whether the risk to be undertaken has a greater than normal risk.

Evidence of greater risk includes the timing and size of cash flows. If they are more variable than normal, greater risk exists, and a higher than normal discount rate should be used in discounting investment cash flows.

A consistent decision rule that uses time value of money is the best method to use when evaluating investments. Overall the NPV method is consistently the best, with the IRR method, except in unusual circumstances, a close second. The NPV and IRR methods usually support the same decision. The payback and accounting ROI methods are weak investment decision rule methods and ordinarily should not be used.

For different types of investments, different methods of ascertaining discount rates are used. Note that any discount rate is generally a proxy for the real or intrinsic rate representing the risk of the project. The discount rate consists of experimental plus judgmental analysis in its final development.

4

Capital Budgeting

Business and other organizations make major expenditures for land, buildings, and equipment to expand or improve operations. In some cases, expansion is accomplished by acquiring existing businesses. Because these various investments are usually of a significant dollar amount, they have profound implications for the long-term success of an organization. Therefore, it is imperative that a sound capital budgeting decision process be followed to determine which investments to make.

Previous chapters dealt with the application of present value concepts and techniques to the valuation of investments and formation of decision rules. Those tools are used in support of the capital budgeting decision process, which has the following steps:

1. Compute the incremental net cash flows associated with the investment alternative or project.
2. Calculate the IRR for each investment and use the IRR decision rule to rank the alternatives.
3. Determine the weighted average cost of capital (COC) for the individual or firm.
4. Compare the IRR with the COC; investments having an IRR greater than the COC are acceptable.
5. Select all investments in rank order (highest IRR to lowest), given the dollar constraints of the budget, to obtain the optimum capital budget.

These steps will be followed for investments in three projects illustrated for J-Co. in this chapter.

INCREMENTAL CASH FLOWS AND
INTERNAL RATE OF RETURN

Incremental after-tax cash flows can be estimated indirectly or directly. Under the indirect method, incremental revenues arising from an investment or project are offset by the incremental expenses and income taxes associated with that investment. The net revenues after tax are then adjusted for noncash charges such as depreciation before being discounted. Under the direct method, after-tax cash flows are estimated explicitly rather than being based on accounting earnings and expenses adjusted for noncash items. In either case the objective is to develop reliable estimates of future cash flows.

To illustrate, assume J-Co. is looking at projects F, G, and H to see which to undertake. F and G are expansion-type projects, and H is a replacement-type project. The analysis for expansion versus replacement projects is different, and a thorough analysis is required to determine the feasibility of the projects.

Project F

Project F requires acquisition of research equipment costing $47,000 with a three-year life and to be depreciated under the accelerated cost recovery system (ACRS). Because J-Co. has never before used research equipment, F is considered an expansion project. The project will bring in additional cash revenue of $41,000 per year for three years, offset by cash operating expenses of $16,000 per year. The income tax rate for the firm will approximate 34 percent. Additional net working capital of $3,000 will be required but will be recovered at the end of the third year. The salvage value of the equipment at the end of Year 3 will be $8,000. The cost to transport the equipment and install it properly will be $3,000.

Given the facts of the case, the steps in the capital budgeting process can be illustrated. The first step is to calculate the total investment necessary for project F. The total in this case is $53,000, consisting of the following: equipment ($47,000), installation and transportation ($2,000 + $1,000), and additional working capital ($3,000).

Note that net working capital includes supplies and other items needed for use with the equipment. However, some credit, such as accounts payable, will be provided. Therefore, current assets (supplies) are offset by current liabilities (accounts payable). If all current asset needs of the project are not met with current liabilities, additional working capital, here $3,000, will be required. Since net working capital is not part of the equipment cost, it is eliminated when calculating depreciation basis. However, transportation and installation costs are considered part of the equipment's cost and are subject to depreciation.

The second step is to calculate annual depreciation. Installation and transportation costs are included in the depreciation base. Those costs ($3,000) plus the cost of the equipment ($47,000) result in a depreciable basis for tax purposes of $50,000. Under the ACRS method, the equipment will not be fully depreciated in three years because ACRS employs use of the half-year convention; that is, no matter when the item is bought in the purchase year, only one-half of the allowable depreciation for the year may be taken. The ACRS percentages and annual depreciation are shown in schedule (4.1). Total depreciation for the three-year period is $46,500, leaving an undepreciated balance or book value of $3,500 at the end of Year 3.

(4.1)

Year	ACRS %	Basis	Depreciation
1	.33	$50,000	$16,500
2	.45	$50,000	22,500
3	.15	$50,000	7,500

Having determined the total investment for project F and allowable depreciation, the third step is to calculate the project's after-tax cash flows (ATCF). Schedule (4.2) illustrates the calculation of ATCF for the three years of the project. (Amounts have been rounded to simplify calculations.)

(4.2)

	Year 1	Year 2	Year 3
Revenues (given)	$41,000	$41,000	$41,000
Operating expenses (given)	(16,000)	(16,000)	(16,000)
Depreciation (Step two)	(16,500)	(22,500)	(7,500)
Earnings before tax	8,500	2,500	17,500
Tax (34%, given)	(2,890)	(850)	(5,950)
Earnings after tax	5,610	1,650	11,550
Add back depreciation	16,500	22,500	7,500
After tax cash flow (ATCF)	$22,110	$24,150	$19,050

The schedule is similar to an income statement and reflects that depreciation is added back to net earnings after taxes because depreciation is a noncash expense. The equipment expenditure was made at the time the investment was made. Annual depreciation provides a tax shield or savings.

To understand better the tax-shielding effect of depreciation, consider Year 2 of schedule (4.2) for investment F. Had depreciation not been deducted, earnings before taxes would have been $25,000 ($41,000 revenue − $16,000 operating expenses); income taxes, $8,500 ($25,000 earnings x 34 percent); and ATCF $16,500 ($25,000 earnings − $8,500 tax). A comparison of ATCF without a depreciation deduction versus ATCF with a depreciation deduction for tax purposes shows that the latter results in an ATCF $7,650 higher ($24,150 − $16,500). The higher amount reflects the tax shield (savings) available by deducting depreciation — that is, $22,500 depreciation x 34% = $7,650.

The fourth step is to compute the after-tax salvage value cash flows (SVCF). The equipment's salvage value (SV) of $8,000 is given. Book value (BV) of $3,500 was noted in conjunction with the second step. Since the salvage value or selling price of the equipment at the end of Year 3 exceeds the book value, J-Co. will have to pay tax on the $4,500 gain ($8,000 − $3,500). Applying the 34 percent tax rate to the gain, taxes equal $1,530, and the SVCF is $6,470 ($8,000 − $1,530). The SVCF calculation is reflected in the equation $SVCF = SV − (SV − BV)$ (T), where T is the tax rate. In this case $SVCF = \$8,000 − (\$8,000 − \$3,500)(.34) = \$6,470$.

Step 5 is to adjust the Year 3 ATCF to reflect the SVCF and recovery of working capital at the end of that year. The final ATCF for Year 3 then becomes $28,520 ($19,050 + $6,470 SVCF + $3,000 working capital recovery). The following time line illustrates the adjusted ATCF for project F for the three-year period:

```
/----------/----------/----------/
0            1          2          3

($53,000)   $21,770   $24,150   $28,520

PV  <-----------------------------
```

Given the ATCF, it is now possible to complete the sixth step in the process: calculation of the IRR for project F. Recall that the IRR is the discount rate, which equates the present value of the cash inflows with the cash outflows. Using present value of 1 factors for the three years at 18 percent, the present value of the ATCF (inflows) equals ($22,110) (.847) + ($24,150) (.718) + ($28,520) (.609) = $53,436. The excess of the present value over the investment cost of $53,000 results in an NPV of $436. The net present value indicates that the IRR is greater than 18 percent.

Since the NPV is small, it is likely that the IRR is between 18 and 20 percent. Using 20 percent factors, the present value is calculated to be $51,691, giving an NPV of –$1,309. Therefore the IRR can now be found by interpolation as follows: the IRR value is $436 ($53,436 – $53,000) of the $1,745 ($53,436 – $51,691) distance between 18 and 20 percent. Therefore, the IRR = ($436 ÷ $1,745) (.02) + .18 = (.025) (.02) + .18 = 18.50 percent = the IRR for project F. Later this IRR will be compared with the cost of capital for J-Co. to determine if the project should be undertaken.

Project G

Project G is also an expansion project, so the incremental cash flows and IRR can be determined by following the same steps taken for project F. The facts for project G are as follows. Operating equipment costing $90,000 will be purchased and will require installation costs of $2,000. The equipment has a five-year life and is to be depreciated under ACRS. Incremental cash revenues will total $56,000 per year for the five-year period, and annual incremental operating expenses will amount to $24,000. The income tax rate will be 34 percent. Net working capital of $4,000 is required and will be recovered at the end of five years. The equipment's estimated salvage value at the end of Year 5 is $12,000.

Recall that the first step in the process is to calculate the net investment in the project, $96,000 in this case ($90,000 for equipment + $2,000 installation cost + $4,000 working capital requirement). The installation cost is included in the depreciation base. The basis for recording depreciation is therefore $92,000 ($90,000 + $2,000). The ACRS percentages and allowable depreciation are summarized in schedule (4.3). Again, because of the half-year convention, the equipment will not be fully depreciated. Total depreciation equals $86,480, leaving a book value at the end of Year 5 of $5,520.

The third step in the process is to estimate the project's ATCF for the five-year period. Incremental cash revenues and expenses plus annual depreciation are used in schedule (4.4), which shows the process for determination of ATCF for each year.

(4.3)

Year	ACRS %	Basis	Depreciation
1	.20	$92,000	$18,400
2	.32	$92,000	$29,440
3	.19	$92,000	$17,480
4	.12	$92,000	$11,040
5	.11	$92,000	$10,120

(4.4)

	Year 1	Year 2	...	Year 5
Revenues	$56,000	$56,000	...	$56,000
Expenses	(24,000)	(24,000)	...	(24,000)
Depreciation	(18,400)	(29,440)	...	(10,120)
Earnings Before Tax	13,600	2,560	...	21,880
Tax (34%)	(4,624)	(871)	...	(7,440)
Profits After Tax	8,976	1,689	...	14,440
Add back depreciation	18,400	19,440	...	10,120
ATCF	$27,376	$31,129	...	$24,560

Again it is necessary to adjust the ATCF of Year 5 by the SVCF arising from disposal of the equipment and for the recovery of working capital. Using the SVCF equation, SVCF = $12,000 − ($12,000 − $5,520$BV$) (.34) = $9,797 = after-tax cash flow arising from sale of the equipment at this $12,000 salvage value. Recall that the $4,000 working capital re-quirement will be recovered at the end of Year 5. The ATCF for Year 5 then becomes $24,560 + $9,797 + $4,000 = $38,357. The ATCF for project G can now be summarized as shown in the following time line:

```
/--------/--------/--------/--------/--------/
0         1        2        3        4        5
($96,000) $27,376 $31,129 $27,063 $24,873 $38,357
PV <---------------------------------------------
```

The final step in the process is to calculate the IRR. By trial and error, the present value of the ATCF can be calculated until it approximates the

$96,000 investment cost. In this case, the present value of the cash flows discounted at 16 percent is above $96,000; and at 18 percent it is below $96,000. The IRR lies between these two percentages. Using interpolation in the same manner as for project F, the IRR is found to be about 16.03 percent. As for project F, the IRR of project G will later be compared to J-Co.'s cost of capital to determine whether the investment should be made.

Project H

This project is a replacement project; a new machine will take the place of an old one. Some of the steps taken in calculating the IRR for project H will vary somewhat from those followed for projects F and G. The major differences result from a need to reduce the net investment in the project for the net proceeds from disposing of the equipment being replaced and to modify ATCF for differences in depreciation available on the old equipment versus the replacement equipment.

The facts for project H are as follows. The firm will replace an old machine that was bought three years ago for $130,000 and that was being depreciated on a straight-line basis over eight years. The estimated salvage value of the old machine when purchased was $10,000, but it can be sold now for $89,000. The cost of the new machine, including transportation and installation, will be $180,000. The firm plans to depreciate the new machine over five years under ACRS. Estimated salvage of the new machine is $15,000 at the end of Year 5. The new machine will reduce annual operating expenses by $26,000, but sales will not be affected. The income tax rate for J-Co. remains 34 percent.

The first step in determining incremental cash flows and the IRR for project H is to calculate the net investment. In this case, preliminary steps must be followed to determine the net cash proceeds from disposing of the old machine. First, the book value is calculated as follows: (cost − salvage) ÷ useful life = annual depreciation — that is, ($130,000 − $10,000) ÷ 8 years = $15,000. Accumulated depreciation for the past three years equals $45,000 ($15,000 x 3 years), and the old machine's book value equals $85,000 ($130,000 − $45,000).

Next, net cash proceeds from selling the old machine at the date of replacement for $89,000 is calculated. Using the SVCF equation, net proceeds = SVCF = $89,000 − ($89,000 − $85,000) (.34) = $87,640 = salvage value of old machine, net of tax on the gain. The net investment in the new machine is therefore $92,360 ($180,000 cost of the new machine − $87, 640 net proceeds from disposal of the old machine).

The next step in the process is to compare depreciation on the old machine with depreciation on the new machine. Annual depreciation for the next five years on the old machine would have continued at $15,000. Therefore, the tax shield provided by depreciation on the new machine will be higher than that provided by the old machine, as illustrated in schedule (4.5).

(4.5)

Year	ACRS%	Basis of New Machine	Depreciation New Machine	Old Machine	Depreciation Increase
1	.20	$180,000	$36,000	$15,000	$21,000
2	.32	180,000	57,600	15,000	42,600
3	.19	180,000	34,200	15,000	19,200
4	.12	180,000	21,600	15,000	6,600
5	.11	180,000	19,800	15,000	4,800

The net increase in depreciation from the old machine to the new machine is shown in the last column on the right. These amounts are used to calculate the tax shield provided by depreciation, that is, the tax savings resulting from deducting depreciation expense in arriving at taxable income. Tax shields are calculated by multiplying the relevant depreciation amounts by the tax rate. In this case, the increase in depreciation afforded by the new machine is multiplied by the 34 percent tax rate given for J-Co., as in schedule (4.6).

(4.6)

Year	Increase in Depreciation	Tax Rate	Depreciation Shield (Tax Savings)
1	$21,000	.34	$ 7,140
2	42,600	.34	14,484
3	19,200	.34	6,528
4	6,600	.34	2,244
5	4,800	.34	1,632

These depreciation shields are then added to savings in operating expenses adjusted for tax to arrive at the ATCF for each of the five years shown in schedule (4.7), where the after-tax rate is $1 - .34 = .66$.

(4.7)

Year	Operating Savings	After-Tax Rate	After-Tax Savings	Depreciation Shield	ATCF
1	$26,000	.66	$17,160	$ 7,140	$24,300
2	26,000	.66	17,160	14,484	31,644
3	26,000	.66	17,160	6,528	23,688
4	26,000	.66	17,160	2,244	19,404
5	26,000	.66	17,160	1,632	18,792

The estimated SVCFs of the new machine in projects F and G were treated as adjustments to the ATCF at the end of the project period when the machines were sold. The same step is followed for project H. Using the SVCF equation, SVCF = $15,000 − ($15,000 − $10,800) (.34) = $13,572, where $15,000 is the salvage value given for H and $10,800 is the book value of the new machine (basis of $180,000 reduced by accumulated depreciation of $169,200) at the end of Year 5. Therefore the adjusted ATCF for Year 5 is $32,364 ($18,792 + $13,572). The following time line summarizes the ATCF for project H:

```
/--------/-------/--------/--------/--------/
  0        1       2        3        4        5

($92,360) $24,300 $31,644 $23,688 $19,404 $32,364

  PV <--------------------------------------------
```

Using the cash flows illustrated in the time line and following the process presented in detail for project F, the IRR for project H is calculated to be 12.93 percent. The reader may want to prove this rate by using the following facts: NPV discounting the ATCF at 12 percent equals $2,117 and at 14 percent equals −$2,442. As with projects F and G, the IRR of 12.93 percent will be compared to the cost of capital for J-Co. in determining whether to invest in H.

The first two steps in the capital budgeting process outlined at the beginning of the chapter have been completed. The ATCFs for projects F, G, and H have been determined, and the IRR for each project has been calculated. The next step is to determine the weighted-average COC for J-Co. so that the IRR of each project can be evaluated. Projects with an IRR greater than the COC are feasible ventures that will add value to J-Co.

WEIGHTED AVERAGE COST OF CAPITAL

Before the weighted average COC can be determined, certain facts about J-Co. are necessary. The capital structure (right-hand side of balance sheet) of J-Co. has $400,000 debt, including short term and long term, and $600,000 equity (capital stock, capital in excess of par, and retained earnings). Additional long-term debt financing can be obtained in the future at 12 percent interest, which is deductible at the tax rate of 34 percent. The compound annual growth in earnings for J-Co. is expected to be 11 percent, and the last dividend paid was $1. The stock of J-Co. is being sold at $17 a share. Additional stock, if sold publicly, would net the firm $13 per share because an underwriting fee of $4 has to be paid. The estimated earnings to be retained from next year's income will total $75,000.

Weights of Debt and Equity

The first step in the determination of COC is to calculate the weights of debt and equity. Since J-Co. has $400,000 debt and $600,000 equity, the proportion of debt to total liabilities and equity is $400,000 divided by $1,000,000, or 40 percent, and the proportion of equity is $600,000 divided by $1,000,000, or 60 percent. It is assumed here that the 40 percent debt–60 percent equity split is optimum for J-Co. (formulas in advanced finance books show how to calculate optimal capital structure for a firm).

Cost of Financing Sources

The second step is to calculate the cost of each source of financing. To determine the after-tax cost of debt, the formula used is interest before tax multiplied by 1 minus the tax rate. The tax adjustment is necessary because interest is deductible for tax purposes, thereby reducing the cost of debt financing. For J-Co. the cost of debt = (interest before tax) $(1 - T) = (12\%) (1 - .34) = .0792$, or 7.92%.

The cost of retained earnings can be determined using the dividend formula: $R = (D \div P) + g$, where

R is the required rate of return for retained earnings,
D is the next expected dividend,
P is the current price of stock, and
g is the growth rate.

Substituting the numbers provided in the facts for J-Co., the equation becomes $R = (\$1.00 \div \$17.00) + 11\% = .17$, or 17.0% (rounded). This number is, in effect, an opportunity cost for investors. If the company cannot reinvest earnings at 17 percent, then earnings should be distributed to shareholders.

Finally, the cost of selling stock publicly is calculated. Making a minor adjustment to the dividend formula by substituting the net price of the stock (selling price minus underwriting fee), the equation becomes $R = (\$1.00 \div \$13.00) + .11 = 19.0\%$ (rounded). Based on the preceding calculations, the cost of each source of financing can be summarized as follows: debt (.0792, or 7.92 percent), retained earnings (.17, or 17.0 percent), and publicly sold stock (.19 or 19.0 percent). These costs are used for calculating the cost of capital.

Alternative Costs of Capital

Given the cost of each source of financing and their respective proportions in the capital structure, the third step in the process is to determine COC under various assumptions. First, the COC is calculated assuming that only retained earnings (to represent 60 percent of the capital budget) and bank debt (to represent 40 percent of the capital budget) are used to finance investments F, G, and H. Recall that the firm's optimal structure was given as 60 percent equity and 40 percent debt. Those proportions should be maintained with new investments so that the firm will continue to have an optimal capital structure. The weighted cost of capital in this case can be stated as $COCRE = (REW)(RER) + (DW)(DR)$, where

$COCRE$ is the weighted average cost of capital with retained earnings,
REW is the weight of retained earnings in the mix of funds,
RER is the rate required on retained earnings,
DW is the weight of debt in the mix of funds, and
DR is the rate required after tax on debt.

Substituting the appropriate weights and required rates of return, the equation becomes $COCRE = (.60)(.17) + (.40)(.0792) = .102 + .0317$

= .1337, or 13.37%. Thus, if J-Co. finances investments with 60 percent equity and 40 percent debt and the equity portion is represented by retained earnings, then the investments have to earn 13.37 percent to cover interest on the debt, subsidized partially through a tax deduction for interest, and to provide the required return on the retained earnings. Returns higher than 13.37 percent on the investments cover the cost of capital and provide additional value to the firm.

A second cost of capital calculation can then be made assuming the stock is sold publicly while maintaining the same 60 percent equity and 40 percent debt weights. The equation for calculating the cost of capital if public stock financing is used is $COCPS = (PSW)(PSR) + (DW)(DR)$, where

$COCPS$ is the weighted average cost of capital with public stock,
PSW is the weight of publicly sold stock in the mix of funds,
PSR is the rate required on publicly sold stock,
DW is the weight of debt in the mix of funds, and
DR is the rate required after tax on debt.

Substituting the required weights and required rates of return, the equation becomes: $COCPS = (.60)(.19) + (.40)(.0724) = .114 + .0317 = .1457$, or 14.57%.

Retained Earnings Budget Support

Having determined the cost of capital for retained earnings (13.37 percent) and the mix of debt and public stock (14.57 percent), it is necessary to see how much of the investment budget will be supported by retained earnings. This fourth step in the process requires that the following calculation be made: retained earnings ÷ weight of equity = retained earnings budget support. Using the facts given for J-Co. the equation is $75,000 ÷ 60% = $125,000. The $75,000 of retained earnings (60 percent) can support debt of $50,000 (40 percent) and still maintain the optimal structure of J-Co. That is, the COCRE will be 13.37 percent up to $125,000 of funds used. Beyond that amount, the cost of capital will rise to 14.57 percent (COCPS) because a mix of public stock funds and debt will be necessary.

COMPARISON OF IRR AND COC

The relationships that exist among the IRRs for projects F, G, and H and the weighted average COC with retained earnings and public stock dictate which projects J-Co. should invest in. Following is a summary of the three projects and their respective internal rates of return:

Project	Investment	IRR
F	$53,000	18.50%
G	96,000	16.03%
H	92,360	12.93%

Note that retained earnings will support investments up to $125,000. However, if total investments exceed that amount, they must generate an IRR in excess of 14.57 percent, the weighted average COC when stock has to be sold publicly (COCPS). For J-Co. projects F and G have an IRR greater than the 14.57 percent cost of financing them. The IRR of H, 12.93 percent, is less than the weighted average COC and should be rejected. The optimal investment (capital) budget for J-Co. is $149,000, which includes the investment of $53,000 in F and $96,000 in G. The retained earnings almost support the total of both projects. Only $24,000 ($149,000 – $125,000) of external capital will be required. The firm may decide to finance the $24,000 temporarily with debt instead of selling a low dollar amount of securities externally. A rigid 60:40 proportion of equity and debt may not necessarily be maintained in the short run.

SUMMARY OF CAPITAL BUDGETING DECISION PROCESS

This chapter illustrated five steps to follow in determining the optimal capital budget of a firm. Using J-Co. as an example, three investment proposals were evaluated. First, the ATCFs on the projects were computed. In the second step, the incremental or after-tax cash flows were used to determine IRRs provided by the projects. Third, the weighted average COCs using only retained earnings versus using retained earnings plus the sale of public stock to finance investments were calculated. The fourth step required that the IRR of each project be compared to the cost of capital percentages. Projects having an IRR greater than the cost of capital were considered acceptable. The final step was determination of the optimal capital budget in dollars. The optimal budget included the sum of the investments whose IRRs exceed the weighted average COC. Note that some firms use COC as a cutoff or hurdle rate to be achieved by investments. Those firms discount ATCF at the COC rate. If the result is a positive NPV, investments are made. Investments are ranked using the performance index illustrated in

Chapter 3. The NPV approach is preferred when investments are mutually exclusive because the investment adding the greatest value (measured as NPV) to the firm will be selected.

The numbers dealt with in capital budgeting cases are based on estimates. The more accurate are the estimates of future incremental cash flows and financing costs, the more accurate the calculated results will be. Not only must quantitative factors be understood and calculated, but there may be times when qualitative factors will be predominant in the decision-making process. A firm whose competitor is installing an innovation that will give it a competitive edge in cost reduction may be forced to invest in a project whose IRR is less than the cost of capital.

Other factors that may be pertinent to capital budgeting decisions reflect the model illustrated in the chapter. Consider the following points. Calculation of ATCF and COC are future oriented. Both amounts should reflect adjustments for inflation and other expectations. Cash flows illustrated for investment projects in this chapter were assumed to occur at the end of each period. Present value tables are available for discounting cash flows assumed to occur uniformly throughout each year.

The net cash outflow required for replacing equipment is influenced by the nature of the replacement. For example, exchanges of similar kinds of equipment are tax free, whereas sales of equipment being replaced result in a gain or loss for tax purposes. The after-tax cash flows associated with the replacement will therefore differ depending on how the replacement is effected. The depreciation tax shield can also be influenced; either straight-line or accelerated depreciation can be used, thereby affecting the timing of the taxes saved by deducting depreciation.

Finally, adjustments may have to be made for inflation as discussed at the end of Chapter 1. It is important to adjust cash flows for inflation if the discount rate is adjusted for inflation, to avoid biased results.

5

Use and Analysis of Debt by Individuals and Businesses

Individuals and businesses frequently make decisions regarding the form and amount of debt they incur. They consider repayment periods and variable versus fixed rates of interest, among other factors. Present value analysis is particularly applicable to all forms of debt because cash outflows are usually known with certainty as to time and amount. In cases where interest rates or payments are not known, it is usually quite easy to determine them by solving the general present value equations provided in Chapter 1.

This chapter examines installment notes, term bonds, zero coupon bonds, and other forms of debt and provides calculations of loan payments, implicit interest rates, and the dollar advantages of early retirement of debt during periods of interest rate changes.

TERM BONDS

It is helpful to begin the discussion of business debt by examining bonds because the interest and principal payments are set by contract. Further, because the bond market is active, it is relatively easy to determine the market value of a company's bonds at virtually any time. Companies issue bonds and other forms of debt to obtain leverage financing. The amount of debt a company incurs is a function of its desired capital structure, cash flow requirements, and other factors related to considerations of risk and return.

Issuance of Bonds

In recent years some companies have begun issuing bonds in denominations of less than the traditional amount of $1,000. Use of smaller denominations, or "baby bonds," enables smaller companies to obtain financing in the bond market more effectively. Regardless of whether a bond is offered in $200, $500, or $1,000 denominations, its issue price is determined by discounting the interest and principal payments due on the bonds to their present value using the market interest rate. Assume, for example, that a company plans to issue term bonds with a $100,000 total face (maturity) value and a stated (contract) annual interest rate of 10 percent. Interest is payable semiannually over the four-year life of the bonds, and the current market rate of interest for bonds in the same risk class is 12 percent. Cash outflows associated with the bonds are illustrated by the following time line:

```
/-------/-------/-------/----... ----/
0       1       2       3    ...   8

      $5,000  $5,000  $5,000   ... $5,000
                                   $100,000

PV  <----------------------------------
```

The $5,000 amounts represent semiannual interest payments due by contract on the bonds ($100,000 face value x 5% semiannual rate), with $100,000 being the principal due at maturity. Because interest is payable semiannually, there are eight time periods, thereby requiring use of a semiannual discount rate in determining the present value of all cash payments due on the bonds. The issue price of the bonds is determined by discounting the cash payments for eight periods at the semiannual market rate of interest, the return required by investors. Both the general equation for calculating the present value of one (for the principal payment) and the equation for the present value of an annuity of 1 (for the interest payments) must be used, as follows.

$$
\begin{array}{llr}
\$100,000\ p8/6 = PV = (\$100,000)(.627) = & \$62,700 \\
\$5,000\ P8/6 = PV = (\$5,000)(6.210) = & 31,050 \\
\text{Issue price (proceeds)} & \$93,750
\end{array}
$$

Because the market interest rate exceeds the stated (contractual) interest rate, the bonds will be issued at a discount from their face value. The issuer therefore incurs interest cost of $5,000 semiannually plus the discount of $6,250 ($100,000 face value − $93,750 issue price) over the life of the bonds, resulting in effective interest expense equal to the 6 percent semiannual market rate. The amortization schedule presented in Table 5.1 shows the effective interest cost for each period over the life of the bonds and can be used by the issuing company in preparing its bond accounting entries.

Note that effective interest cost each period is calculated by multiplying the preceding period's carrying value by the 6 percent effective semiannual interest rate. The difference between effective interest and cash interest is reflected through periodic amortization of the $6,250 discount on the bonds. The amortized amount also increases the carrying value of the bonds. At any point in time, the carrying value equals the present value of remaining payments due on the bonds discounted at the 6 percent semiannual rate.

Retirement of Bonds before Maturity

A bond issuer's effective interest amounts and periodic bond-carrying amounts do not change from the information on the bond amortization schedule during the life of the bonds; all cash flows, both proceeds

TABLE 5.1
Amortization Schedule, Four Year, Ten Percent Bonds, Issued at Twelve Percent Yield

n	Effective Semiannual Interest	Cash Interest	Discount Ammortization	Carrying Value
0	-	-	-	$93,750
1	$5,625	$5,000	$ 625	94,375
2	5,663	5,000	663	95,038
3	5,702	5,000	702	95,740
4	5,744	5,000	744	96,484
5	5,789	5,000	789	97,273
6	5,836	5,000	836	98,109
7	5,886	5,000	886	98,995
8	6,005*	5,000	1,005*	100,000
Total	$46,250	$40,000	$6,250	

* rounded $65 to correct for rounding of present value factor

and payments, were established at the issue date. However, the market rate of interest for the bonds will fluctuate to reflect bond market conditions. As a consequence, the market price of the bonds will inevitably differ from the issuer's carrying amount at any time. In many cases, market interest rates rise, resulting in bond market values below carrying amounts.

For example, assume that two years after issuance, that is, at the end of Period 4 on the amortization schedule (Table 5.1), the market interest rate rises to 14 percent. The market price at this time will equal the present value of the maturity value and remaining interest payments on the bonds, discounted at a 7 percent semiannual rate for the remaining four time periods (8 periods – 4 periods). Using the general present value equations, the market price is calculated as follows:

$$\$100{,}000 \; p4/7 = PV = (\$100{,}000) \; (.763) = \quad \$76{,}300$$
$$\$5{,}000 \; P4/7 = PV = (\$5{,}000) \; (3.387) = \quad 16{,}935$$
$$\text{Market price} \qquad\qquad \$93{,}235$$

A comparison of the market price with the bond-carrying amount at the end of Period 4 shows that the issuer can recognize a gain of $3,249 ($96,484 carrying value – $93,235 market price) by reacquiring its own bonds in the market and retiring them. Many major corporations have reported gains of several million dollars arising through such reacquisitions before maturity. Cash for reacquisitions can come from issuance of new debt or equity securities by a firm but often at much higher interest rates. Of course, if market interest rates decline, the market bond price will exceed the carrying amount, forcing an issuer to recognize a loss if bonds are reacquired. In the latter case, however, issuers can issue new bonds at lower interest rates and reduce their periodic cash outflows for interest.

Some companies may take advantage of interest rate changes to replace debt financing with equity financing to improve their ratio of debt to equity. Whether companies should refund bonds — that is, replace an old issue with a new issue when interest rates decline — is essentially a capital budgeting problem requiring analysis similar to that for an equipment replacement decision.

Bond Refundings

Companies should consider replacing (refunding) old issues of bonds with new issues when interest rates decline. A reduction in overall financing costs should result in lower financial risk and therefore a higher value for a company. Bond refundings are essentially capital budgeting problems that require use of discounted cash flow calculations. The following example illustrates the present value analysis required for making a refunding decision.

A company has outstanding twenty-year bonds with a face value of $100,000 and annual interest payments of 12 percent, or $12,000. The bonds were issued at their face (maturity) value five years ago and are callable at 103 ($103,000). A new issue of $100,000 bonds with a fifteen-year term (same as the remaining term on the old bonds) can be issued at their face value with an annual interest cost of 10 percent, or $10,000. The call premium is deductible for income tax purposes at the company's average tax rate of 40 percent. The net present value calculations illustrated for equipment acquisition and replacement decisions in Chapter 4 apply to this bond refunding case.

The NPV model first requires calculation of the net cash outlay to effect the refunding — in this case, the after-tax cost of the $3,000 call premium, or $1,800 ($3,000 − $1,200 tax savings). Second, the after-tax incremental cash flow savings (ATCF) arising from the difference in interest between the old and new bond issue must be calculated. Annual after-tax cash outflow for interest on the old bonds is $7,200 ($12,000 interest − $4,800 tax savings) and for the new bonds is $6,000 ($10,000 interest − $4,000 tax savings). Therefore, the incremental cash flow is a savings of $1,200 ($7,200 − $6,000).

Third, the ATCF must be discounted to its present value at an appropriate discount rate. In equipment acquisitions, a company's after-tax cost of capital is used as the discount rate to reflect both risk and the hurdle rate to be exceeded if the company's investment returns are to exceed financing costs. In the bond refunding example, however, the after-tax cost of the new bonds should be used as the discount rate. Unlike equipment acquisition decisions, where future incremental cash flows are based on assumptions and estimates, incremental interest cash flows for the bonds are known with certainty and are essentially risk free. Therefore they can be discounted at a lower interest rate. The after-tax interest cost of the bonds is 6 percent (new rate of 10% − 4% tax savings). The cash flows for this example are presented in the following time line:

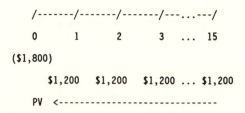

```
/-------/-------/-------/---...---/
0       1       2       3  ...  15
($1,800)

      $1,200   $1,200   $1,200 ... $1,200

PV  <----------------------------
```

The solution to the refunding problem then becomes: present value of incremental cash flows = *PV,* where

$$PV = \$1{,}200\ P15/6 = (\$1{,}200)\ (9.712) = \quad \$11{,}654$$
$$\text{Net cash outlay} \qquad\qquad 1{,}800$$
$$\text{Net present value} \qquad\quad \$9{,}854$$

Since the present value of the interest savings exceeds the cost to effect the refunding, the new bonds should be issued.

A fuller analysis of the refunding question requires consideration of additional net interest cost that may arise if the new bonds are issued before the old bonds are retired. Further, costs of issuing the new bonds and unamortized issue costs associated with the old bonds should be considered. Both types of cost can be considered adjustments to the calculation of net cash outlay. For example, assume that unamortized issue costs on the old bonds amounted to $1,500 and were being amortized at the rate of $100 per year. Issue costs for the new bonds total $2,250 and will be amortized at the rate of $150 per year. Also assume that issuance of the new bonds precedes the call of the old bonds by two months and that proceeds of the new issue will be invested to earn $1,300 during that period. Interest on the old bonds for the two-month period is $2,000. Cash flows associated with these items occur as follows (cash outflows in brackets):

```
/-------/-------/-------/---... ---/
0       1       2       3  ...   15
($1,200)

$780

$600   ($40)   ($40)   ($40) ... ($40)

($2,250) $60    $60     $60  ...  $60

PV  <----------------------------
```

The $1,200 represents the after-tax cost of two months' interest on the old bonds after the new bonds are issued ($2,000 interest – $800 tax savings). After-tax interest earnings arising from investing the proceeds of the new bond issue during that same period are reflected by the $780 ($1,300 earnings – $520 additional tax). If the old bonds are refunded, the $1,500 unamortized issue cost becomes immediately tax deductible and saves $600 ($1,500 x 40% tax rate). However, that amount would have been saved over the next fifteen years had the old bonds remained outstanding; therefore, the $600 savings must be reduced by the present value of the $40 annual savings that otherwise would have been available ($100 amortization per year x 40% tax rate). New bond issue costs are $2,250 and are deductible for tax purposes over the life of the new bond issue. Therefore, annual cash savings in taxes of $60 will arise from amortization at the rate of $150 per year. Discounting these additional cash flows to their present value at the semiannual rate of 6 percent results in an increase to net cash outlay of $1,876, calculated as follows: $780 + $600 – $1,200 – $2,250 – ($40 *P*15/6) + ($60 *P*15/6). Substituting present value factors, the equation becomes $780 + $600 – $1,200 – $2,250 – ($40 x 9.712) + ($60 x 9.712) = –$1,876. Using the adjustment to net cash outlay, the NPV calculation appears as follows:

Present value	$11,654
Net cash outlay ($1,800 + $1,876)	3,676
Net present value	$ 7,978

Therefore, the bonds should still be refunded.

ZERO COUPON BONDS

A popular alternative to conventional term bonds is zero coupon bonds on which no periodic interest payments are made. Instead the issuer's cost is reflected solely in the discounted price at issuance. For example, if a $1,000 ten-year zero coupon bond is issued when the market interest rate is 12 percent, the issue price will be $1,000 discounted at 12 percent for ten years. The issue price calculation reflects the cash flow illustrated in the following time line:

```
/-----/-----/-----/---... ---/
0     1     2     3   ...   10
                           $1,000
PV  <--------------------------
```

Using the general equation for calculating the present value of 1, the calculation becomes: $PV = \$1,000\, p10/12 = (\$1,000)\,(.322) = \$322$. The difference between the issue price of $322 and the maturity value of $1,000 represents the effective interest cost to the issuer. Interest effectively accumulates at 12 percent on the $322 proceeds over the ten-year life of the bonds, resulting in an obligation at maturity equal to the face value of the bonds.

If interest rates are expected to decline, a company should postpone a bond issue because proceeds will increase as rates fall; the lower discount rate results in a higher present value. Conversely, higher interest rates will result in lower present values and, hence, lower proceeds. The advantage to a company of issuing zero coupon bonds is that the cost of the bonds to an investor is significantly less than the face value, thereby making the bonds affordable to a larger number of investors. The dollar amount of effective annual interest on zero coupon bonds is deductible for tax purposes each year by the issuer and reportable as income each year by the investor.

LONG-TERM NOTES

Notes payable are essentially like bonds in that they are contractual obligations to pay specific amounts of interest and principal over a period of time. However, notes are frequently issued in smaller total dollar amounts and for shorter time periods; the market for notes is not as broad as for bonds; notes do not normally have to be registered with the Securities and Exchange Commission; repayment terms on notes frequently require payments of both principal and interest; and notes may include variable interest rates.

Determining Interest and Principal Payments

Despite differences that may exist between a given note and a bond obligation, proceeds, repayment terms, and so on for both are based directly on present value calculations because cash flows are certain with respect to time and amount. Specialized loan payment books used by employees of lending institutions, automobile dealerships, and others to determine monthly loan payments assuming various interest rates, amounts financed, and repayment periods are developed using present value calculations.

Assume a two-year installment note is issued in exchange for an item of equipment costing $16,000. The stated interest rate is 12 percent, and monthly payments include both principal and interest. The monthly payment amounts are determined by solving the equation for the present value of an annuity of 1 with monthly payments of X. Because payments are monthly, the factor for twenty-four monthly periods and 1 percent interest (12% annual rate ÷ 12 months) must be used. The equation then is X $P24/1 = PV = \$16,000$. Substituting the $P24/1$ factor, $PV = (\$X) (21.243) = \$16,000$, and $X = \$753$ (rounded to the nearest dollar). Each payment of $753 includes principal and interest. One percent interest on the $16,000 financed the first month is $160 ($16,000 x 1%), with the remaining $593 portion of the payment applicable to principal, leaving an unpaid balance of $15,407 ($16,000 − $593). The second month's interest will be calculated on the $15,407 balance at the monthly rate, that is ($15,407 x 1 percent) = second month's interest = $154. A computer can be used to prepare a loan amortization schedule showing the principal and interest portion of each of the remaining payments. The schedule can be used to determine the unpaid principal balance or payoff amount at any point during the term of the loan.

Imputing Interest

Noninterest-bearing notes are sometimes exchanged for equipment or other assets. A problem arises in that it is customary to charge interest whenever amounts are financed for more than one or two months. In other cases, a note may include a stated amount of interest, but the rate is well below the market rate. In either case, it is necessary to impute effective interest cost for income tax purposes and so that the true cost of the asset acquired can be determined. The following examples illustrate how to impute interest.

Assume a start-up business is interested in buying equipment from a manufacturer. The latter is willing to accept a $20,000 down payment at the time of sale plus a noninterest-bearing note for $30,000 due in three years. If the buyer's incremental cost of borrowing a similar amount from a financial institution is 18 percent, that rate should be used to impute interest on the note. The only payment required on the note is the $30,000 face amount due at maturity. Solving the general equation for calculating the present value of 1, the effective dollar amount of financing provided by the manufacturer is determined as follows: $30,000 $p3/18 = PV$ = ($30,000) (.609) = $18,270. The cost of the equipment is therefore $38,270 ($20,000 down payment + the $18,270 present value of the note), not $50,000. The buyer should recognize interest over the three-year term of the note for the $11,730 difference between the face amount and the present value of the note. Table 5.2 illustrates the accumulation of interest each year. Observe that accumulation of interest at the market rate on the initial amount financed results in a maturity value equal to the $30,000 face amount of the note. The annual amount of interest is deductible for tax purposes.

Early Repayment and Refinancing of Notes

Periods of declining interest rates present borrowers an opportunity to refinance existing loans at lower rates. As with bonds, however, costs associated with refinancing loans before maturity may exceed interest savings. For example, if there are prepayment penalties on an old loan and updated credit review or other costs on a new loan, the costs may exceed the present value of interest savings gained from refinancing. The present value analysis illustrated for bond refundings is equally applicable to decisions to refinance loans. Readers are encouraged to complete such analyses to determine whether specific loans should be refinanced or repaid before maturity.

TABLE 5.2
Amortization Schedule, Noninterest-Bearing Note, Interest Imputed at Eighteen Percent

n	Interest Expense	Interest Paid	Carrying Value of Note
0	-	-	$18,270
1	3,289	0	21,559
2	3,881	0	25,440
3	4,560*	0	30,000

* rounded $19 to correct for rounding of present value factor

Adjustable Rate Loans

Adjustable interest rate loans appeal to both lenders and borrowers. Lenders avoid being locked into comparatively low interest returns if interest rates rise during the term of a loan. Borrowers benefit by having lower loan payment amounts initially than might otherwise be available, and if interest rates do not fluctuate, the benefits may continue throughout the term of a loan. Whether a borrower should elect an adjustable rate loan in lieu of a fixed rate depends on the loan terms and the borrower's expectations concerning future interest rates. Present value analysis can be used to determine whether the cost of a fixed rate loan is greater than or less than the cost of an adjustable rate loan. (Chapter 7 presents a detailed comparison of a fixed rate mortgage with an adjustable rate mortgage.)

AUTOMOBILE FINANCING

Although the discussion here focuses on loan repayment terms for automobile purchases, the material applies to the repayment of any other installment debt, individual or business.

As the cost of many automobiles has more than doubled over the past ten years, consumers have sought to finance their purchases over extended repayment periods. Loans are now commonly paid off over four to five years rather than three to three and one-half years. The dollar benefit of extending repayment periods decreases at an increasing rate, as illustrated in the example (5.3).

Repayment Period Selection

Assume a new car is purchased at a cost of $15,000. After making a 20 percent down payment ($3,000 in this case), the purchaser has to finance the balance of $12,000. The monthly payment due on a thirty-six-month installment note at 12 percent interest is $399 (Table 5.3). If the loan is extended to sixty months, the payment is reduced by $114 ($399 − $285). However, approximately 70 percent of the decrease — that is, $83 of the $114 — is attributable to the extension from thirty-six months to forty-eight months. Extending the loan twelve more periods, from forty-eight to sixty months, results in an additional decrease in monthly payments of only $31. The cost to the purchaser of the $31 monthly reduction in payments is additional interest of $1,932, computed by comparing total payments for sixty months (60 x $285) with total

TABLE 5.3
Installment Loan Payment Schedule, Alternative Interest Rates and Terms, Financing of $12,000

Annual Interest Rate	Monthly Payments			
	24 months	36 months	48 months	60 months
6%	$ 532	$ 365	$ 282	$ 251
12%	565	399	316	285
18%	599	434	352	321

* based on factors not in the appendix

payments for forty-eight months (48 x $316). Therefore, a purchaser should probably opt for a forty-eight-month rather than sixty-month repayment period when monthly payment amounts for even shorter term loans are unmanageable.

Effect of Interest

The dollar change in payments between periods remains the same regardless of changes in the interest rate (Table 5.3). That is, there is about a $166 difference in payments for twenty-four-month versus thirty-six-month repayment periods regardless of whether the interest rate is 6, 12, or 18 percent. Further, the difference in payments for a twenty-four-month, 6 percent loan versus a 12 percent loan is the same as the difference in payments for a thirty-six-month loan at those two interest rates. These mathematical relationships make comparisons of the effects of interest rate and repayment term changes relatively straightforward. Notice too the dramatic effect of interest rates on a relatively short loan period of thirty-six months. In Table 5.3 it can be seen that monthly payments on the $12,000 loan are about $70 greater at an 18 percent versus 6 percent financing rate.

Cash Rebate versus Reduced Interest Rate Options

The automobile industry now makes extensive use of cash rebate and interest rate incentive options to increase sales. Present value analysis can be used to guide a purchaser in the choice of options. Consider the following example.

A purchaser must choose between a $400 cash rebate and a 6 percent interest rate in an automobile purchase requiring $12,000 of financing. If the cash rebate is chosen, the purchase will have to be financed at the current 12 percent market rate of interest. In either case the loan repayment period will be thirty-six months. These terms enable us to use the payment amounts illustrated in Table 5.3. The choice, then, is a $365 monthly payment and no cash rebate if the interest incentive option is selected versus a $399 payment and $400 cash rebate if the latter is selected. If the present value of the $34 monthly savings in payments ($399 − $365) exceeds the $400 rebate, the purchaser should choose the interest rate option. The monthly savings should be discounted at 12 percent, the current market interest rate, as follows: $34 $P36/1$ = PV = present value of the monthly savings in loan payments, where $P36/1$ is the present value factor for an ordinary annuity of thirty-six periods at a 1 percent monthly rate. Substituting the appropriate factor, the equation becomes ($34) (30.108) = PV = $1,024. Since the $1,024 present value of monthly savings exceeds the $400 rebate, the rebate should be rejected. Whether rebates should always be rejected depends on their size in relation to the dollar amount being financed and the interest rate options available.

Lease versus Purchase of Automobile

Another approach to gaining lower monthly payments is to lease rather than purchase an automobile, a topic discussed in the following chapter.

6

Use and Analysis of Leases by Individuals and Businesses

Like bonds and notes, the cash payments under lease contracts are often known in advance in terms of time and amount. Lease payments, interest costs, implicit interest rates, and other lease-related amounts can be calculated in a manner analogous to the techniques used for bonds and notes. Among the questions raised concerning leases are those involving the issues of leasing versus purchasing, whether leases should be capitalized in financial statements, and whether there is a tax advantage of leasing assets under a capital lease versus an operating lease arrangement.

LEASE TERMINOLOGY AND PRINCIPLES

Leasing is a method of financing the use of assets that can be tailored to a variety of circumstances and conditions. Illustrations presented in this chapter assume the use of capital lease arrangements unless stated otherwise.

Operating versus Capital Lease Arrangements

Under operating lease arrangements, a lessee pays for the right to use an asset for a period of time, after which the asset reverts to the lessor. The lessee gains no ownership interest in the leased asset and normally incurs none of the usual costs of ownership such as property taxes and insurance. Typical examples of operating lease arrangements include short-term car and truck rentals, apartment or office space rentals, and various other short- and long-term rentals where lessees use assets for periods much shorter than the asset lives or where they gain no equity interest in the assets.

Capital leases are characterized by a lessee's acquisition of an equity or ownership interest. Lessees in those cases normally pay property tax, insurance, and other costs coincident with ownership of assets and often gain title to the assets either outright or upon payment of an option or renewal amount, or they have the right to use the assets for virtually all of their useful lives. Specific criteria used in determining capital versus operating leases for accounting purposes are contained in professional accounting pronouncements. Typical examples of capital lease arrangements include acquisitions of assets from dealers where lessees gain direct financing of the acquisition through a lease arranged with a bank or other financial institution, a lessee's acquisition of equipment directly from a manufacturer under a long-term lease contract, and other situations where lessees gain right to use assets for virtually their entire useful lives.

The distinction between capital and operating leases is important. A capital lease is, in substance, no different from an installment note payable. Therefore many of the principles that apply to notes apply equally to leases.

Determining Lease Payments

Calculation of lease payments parallels the determination of payments due under an installment loan. The present value of lease payments should equal the fair value of the asset being leased. From the lessor's viewpoint, the lease payments should be sufficient to provide a market interest rate of return. If the lessor is a dealer or a manufacturer of equipment, the lease payments must also provide for the normal profit applicable to sales of such assets. Unless a lessee knows the fair value of the asset leased or the interest rate implicit in the lease payments charged by the lessor, the lessee should discount lease payments at the incremental borrowing rate. Consider the following examples.

Assume a company wants to acquire equipment from a dealer at a negotiated price of $20,000. To finance the acquisition, the lessee obtains 100 percent financing from a local bank, providing for annual year-end lease payments for five years. In addition the bank requires the lessee to reimburse the bank for the latter's payment of annual property taxes and insurance, estimated at $400. The bank will pay the dealer $20,000 for the equipment and will set the lease payments at an amount sufficient to provide a 12 percent return.

The annual $400 payment to reimburse the bank for insurance and property taxes, referred to as *executory costs,* are not included in the determination of lease payments. The annual lease payments can be determined using the general equation for the present value of an annuity of 1. In this case the equation is $PV = \$X\ P5/12 = \$20,000 = (\$X)$ (3.605); $\$X = \$5,548$ = annual lease payment. The following time line illustrates the lessor's cash flows:

```
       /--------/--------/--------/--------/--------/
       0        1        2        3        4        5
    ($20,000)  $5,548   $5,548   $5,548   $5,548   $5,548
       PV  <-----------------------------------------
```

The difference between the bank's $20,000 payment to the dealer and its $27,740 ($5,548 x 5) in receipts from the lessee represents the 12 percent interest return to the bank. The annual interest earned by the bank, and recognized as expense by the lessee, can be determined by preparing an amortization schedule similar to that required for a fixed rate installment note.

If the bank required lease payments at the beginning of each year, the equation for calculating the present value of an annuity due would have to be used for determining the annual lease payments. The first year's payment can be treated as a down payment, leaving the amount of financing provided by the bank equal to $20,000 minus the first year's payment. Using $\$X$ to represent the annual payments, the following time line reflects the annuity due example from the lessor's viewpoint:

```
       /-----/-----/-----/-----/-----/
       0     1     2     3     4     5
    ($20,000)
       $X    $X    $X    $X    $X
       PV  <---------------------------
```

The general equation for the calculation of the present value of an annuity of 1 can be modified to reflect the annuity due as follows: $PV = \$X + \$X\ P4/12 = \$20,000 = \$X + (\$X)\ (3.037) = (\$X)\ (4.037)$; $\$X = \$4,954$. The first lease payment does not have to be discounted because the bank receives it at the time the lease agreement is entered into.

The lower lease payment amount reflects the fact that the bank recovers its investment sooner under the annuity due arrangement and hence can still earn a 12 percent return despite the lower payments.

As a separate case, assume that the lessee company in the illustration negotiates a lease contract directly with the equipment dealer. Without agreeing on a price for the equipment, the dealer offers the company the option to acquire the equipment by entering into a five-year lease with annual year-end lease payments, excluding executory costs, of $5,548. Not knowing either the dealer's implicit interest return (assumed to be, like the bank's, 12 percent) or the negotiated price the dealer would accept (assumed to be $20,000 as in the previous illustration), the lessee company must determine the amount at which to record the equipment acquisition. The appropriate discount rate to be used by the lessee is the rate it would have to pay if it borrowed money under an installment loan arrangement to acquire the asset. Assuming the borrowing rate, referred to as the *incremental borrowing rate,* is 10 percent, the capitalizable value of the equipment from the lessee's viewpoint is calculated as follows: PV = $5,548 $P5/10$ = ($5,548) (3.791) = $21,032 = capitalizable value or cost of equipment. The lessee should discount the lease payments at the lessor's implicit rate only if it is less than the incremental borrowing rate and known to the lessee.

Effect of Residual Values or Option Prices on Lease Payments

Previous examples assumed that the total cost of leased equipment was to be recovered by the lessor through periodic lease payments. In many cases, however, lease contracts provide lessees the option to purchase the leased equipment at a set price at the end of the lease term or require lessees to guarantee the residual value of the leased item. Option prices are sometimes set considerably below the expected residual values of equipment at the end of lease terms to entice lessees to purchase assets at that time. The existence of guaranteed residual value clauses, bargain purchase options, and similar provisions affects calculations of lease payments and capitalizable values of assets acquired in lease transactions.

Assume a lessor owns equipment that cost $24,000 and has a seven-year life. The equipment is to be leased to a company for a five-year period, at which time it is expected to have a value (residual or market value) of $8,000. Terms of the lease require that the lessee guarantee the residual value. Annual year-end lease payments are calculated to provide the lessor with a 10 percent return on the amount invested in the equipment. The $24,000 investment cost should be reduced by the present value of the residual amount that will be recovered when the lessor sells the equipment at the end of the lease term or leases it to someone else for the last two years of the equipment's life. That is, the lessor need recover only the difference between the equipment's cost and the present value of its residual amount from the lessee during the five-year lease period.

The present value of the residual amount is calculated using the general equation for the present value of 1, as follows: $PV = \$8,000$ $p5/10 = (\$8,000) (.621) = \$4,968$. Therefore, the net amount to be recovered through the five-year lease payments is $19,032 ($24,000 − $4,968). Use of the general equation for calculating the present value of an annuity of 1 results in $PV = \$19,032 = \$X\ P5/10 = (\$X) (3.791)$; $X = \$5,020$, where X represents the annual year-end lease payments. The following time line illustrates the cash flows from the viewpoint of the lessor:

```
    /-------/--------/--------/--------/-------/
    0       1        2        3        4       5

($24,000)

                                          $8,000

      $5,020   $5,020   $5,020   $5,020   $5,020

   PV  <----------------------------------------
```

An amortization schedule showing the 10 percent return earned each year by the lessor should include the $8,000 residual value at the end of Year 5 plus the $5,000 interest.

From the lessee's viewpoint, the equipment is not capitalizable as an asset because it reverts to the lessor at the end of the lease term. Therefore, the lease would be treated as an operating lease, providing annual rent expense deductions of $5,020 for income tax purposes. The lessee should consider whether the residual value will likely equal or exceed the guaranteed amount before accepting the terms of the lease. The lessee will be obligated to make up any deficiency.

If the lease provided instead for an option purchase price of $3,000 at the end of the lease term and the residual value was still estimated to be $8,000, the equipment would be capitalizable. The presumption is that the lessee will not forego the opportunity to purchase the asset at the bargain price and to obtain title to the equipment. The lessee is effectively buying the equipment for $24,000, using the lease to finance the acquisition. The lessor in this case has to calculate the lease payments to reflect a cash inflow of $3,000 instead of $8,000 at the end of Year 5. Assume that 10 percent is an appropriate discount rate for both the lessor and lessee. The lessor will recover its $24,000 investment through receipt of the annual lease payments plus the virtually certain payment of $3,000 by the lessee at the end of Year 5. The lessor calculates the lease payments by first deducting the $1,863 present value of the option price ($3,000 $p5/10 = PV = $ [$3,000] [.621] = $1,863) from the $24,000. The lease payments must therefore provide a 10 percent return on the lessor's net investment of $22,137 ($24,000 − $1,863). Using the general equation for the present value of an annuity, the lease payments are calculated as follows: $PV = $22,137 = $X P5/10 = ($X) (3.791)$, and X = the lease payments = $5,839.

Implicit Interest Rates

In a previous example, it was assumed that a lessee company did not know the negotiated price a dealer would accept for an item of equipment, so the capitalizable value had to be determined using the lessee's incremental borrowing rate. If, however, the market price for an item of equipment is firmly established and is not subject to negotiation, a lessee company can determine the interest rate implicit in lease payments, regardless of their amount or the payment pattern. To determine the implicit interest rate (like IRR discussed in Chapter 3), a lessee discounts periodic lease payments at the rate necessary to have their present value equal the market price of the equipment.

To illustrate the calculation of implicit interest, a ten-year lease arrangement between an equipment dealer and a purchaser is assumed. The purchaser (lessee) agrees to make annual year-end lease payments, excluding executory costs, of $19,172. The fair market value of the equipment is $100,000. The rate required to discount the annual payments to a present value of $100,000 is the interest rate implicit in the lease. A time line illustrating the lease payments to be discounted and their present value (the market value of the equipment) follows:

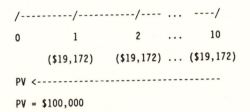

```
/----------/-----------/---- ... ----/
0          1           2     ...    10
    ($19,172)     ($19,172) ... ($19,172)

PV <-----------------------------------

PV = $100,000
```

The general equation for calculating the present value of an annuity of 1 can be used to determine the implicit interest rate. In this case the equation is $PV = \$100,000 = \$19,172\ P10/i$, where i is the interest rate implicit in the lease contract. Solving for i, the equation becomes $PV = \$100,000 = (\$19,172)\ (P10/i\ \text{factor})$. Dividing $100,000 by $19,172, the $P10/i$ factor is calculated to be 5.216. Referring to the period 10 line of the "Present Value of an Annuity of $1" table, the 5.216 factor is found under the 14 percent column. Thus the implicit rate of interest is 14 percent. Had the factor been between two of the table factors, calculation of the implicit interest rate would have required interpolation.

Assume in the preceding illustration that the $19,172 lease payments were due at the beginning of each year but that all other facts, including the $100,000 equipment market value, were unchanged. The payment pattern is an annuity due, and the equation used to solve for the implicit rate would have to be stated as follows: $PV = \$100,000 = \$19,172 + \$19,172\ P9/i$. The equation reflects the fact that the first payment does not have to be discounted. Also the remaining payments are simply an ordinary annuity for nine periods (ten periods minus the first payment). The equation then becomes $PV = \$80,828$ (the $100,000 market value minus the first $19,172 payment) $= \$19,172\ P9/i$, and the $P9/i$ factor is 4.216. Referring to the period 9 line of the "Present Value of an Annuity of $1" table, the factor is found between 18 and 20 percent. The rate, determined by interpolation, is about one-third the distance between the two rates, or approximately 18.6 percent.

The income tax effects of capital versus operating leases are discussed in the next section.

LEASE VERSUS PURCHASE DECISIONS

A lease versus purchase decision is based on a prior decision of whether to acquire an asset for use. The acquisition decision can be made using the discounted cash flow model discussed and illustrated in

Chapter 4. Once a business decides to acquire an asset, it must decide how to finance the acquisition. If cash or proceeds from the issuance of stock are not used, the firm must borrow. A capital lease financing arrangement is, in substance, the same as a loan or a note payable. The lease versus purchase decision therefore becomes a question of whether to finance an acquisition with debt (long-term note or capital lease) or with an operating lease.

Business Example

Assume A-Co. has equipment that sells for $60,000 and has an after-tax salvage value at the end of four years of $10,000. B-Co. completes a capital budgeting analysis and decides to acquire equipment for use in operations over the next four years. It can obtain the equipment from A-Co. by signing either of two leases. Under the first arrangement, B-Co. can use the equipment for four years, guarantee the residual value, and agree to return the asset to A-Co. Under the second arrangement, B-Co. has the option to purchase the equipment at the end of the four-year lease term at the bargain price of $2,000.

The second arrangement results in a capital lease, requiring B-Co. to recognize the acquisition as a purchased asset to be depreciated. Annual lease payments include principal and tax-deductible interest elements. The first arrangement is an operating lease that results in tax-deductible lease rental payments each year. The lessor calculates the lease payments as follows, assuming a 10 percent return is required.

For the first arrangement, X $P4/10 = \$60,000 - \$10,000$ $p4/10$ (investment in equipment minus amount recovered at the end of the lease). Solving the equation, $(\$X)$ $(3.170) = \$60,000 - (\$10,000)$ $(.683) = \$53,170$; $\$X = \$16,773$ = lease payment. In the second arrangement, $\$X$ $P4/10 + \$2,000$ $p4/10 = \$60,000 = (\$X)$ $(3.170) + (\$2,000)$ $(.683) = (\$X)$ $(3.170) = \$58,634$; $\$X = \$18,497$ = lease payment.

An amortization schedule for the capital lease is presented in Table 6.1. Note that the Year 4 lease payment includes the $2,000 option price. Interest expense in the schedule plus annual depreciation expense represent tax-deductible expenses for B-Co. Assuming that B-Co. can realize the $10,000 salvage value, annual straight-line depreciation expense will be $12,500 [($60,000 - $10,000) ÷ 4 years].

Discounted amounts of after-tax cash flows for the capital lease arrangement are presented in Table 6.2. The tax rate is assumed to be 40 percent, and the discount rate used is the after-tax cost of debt financing of 6 percent (a low discount rate is used because the cash flows are

TABLE 6.1
Amortization Schedule, B-Co. Capital Lease

Period	Lease Payment	10% Interest	Principal	Balance
0	$ -	$ -	$ -	$60,000
1	18,497	6,000	12,497	47,503
2	18,497	4,750	13,747	33,756
3	18,497	3,376	15,121	18,635
4	20,497	1,862*	18,635	-0-
Total	$75,988	$15,988	$60,000	

*rounded $2 to correct for rounding of present value factors

TABLE 6.2
Discounted After-tax Cash Flows, B-Co. Capital Lease

	Year One	Year Two	Year Three	Year Four	Total
Tax Deductible Expenses:					
Depreciation	$12,500	$12,500	$12,500	$12,500	
Interest (Table 6-1)	6,000	4,750	3,376	1,862	
Total	18,500	17,250	15,876	14,362	
Income Tax Rate	x .40	x .40	x .40	x .40	
Tax Savings	(7,400)	(6,900)	(6,350)	(5,745)	
Lease Payments	18,497	18,497	18,497	20,497	
After-Tax Cash Flow	11,097	11,597	12,147	14,752	
Six Percent Discount Factor	.943	.890	.840	.792	
Present Value	$10,464	$10,321	$10,203	$11,684	$42,672

highly probable). The total present value of the after-tax cash outflows of B-Co. under the capital lease arrangement is $34,752 ($42,672 total present value from Table 6.2 minus $7,920, the present value of the $10,000 after-tax salvage value discounted at 6 percent).

Under the operating lease arrangement, the annual lease payment of $16,773 will be fully deductible for tax purposes as equipment rental expense. The annual after-tax cash outflow for the operating lease is an annuity determined by deducting the annual tax savings (40% x the lease payment) from the annual lease payment as follows: $16,773 lease payment – $6,709 tax savings ($16,773 x 40%) = after-tax cash flow = $10,064. The present value of the after-tax cash flow is determined by using the general equation for the present value of an ordinary annuity: $10,064 $P4/6 = PV$ = ($10,064) (3.465) = $34,872 = present value of the cost of the operating lease. Since this amount is $120 greater than the total present value of cash outflows under the capital lease arrangement, the latter should be chosen.

In Table 6.2, note that the dollar amount of expense deductible each year under the capital lease arrangement ranges from a high of $18,500 in Year 1 to a low of $14,362 in Year 4. By comparison the annual tax-deductible expense under the operating lease is the annual payment of $16,773. The higher lease payment under the capital lease ($18,497) is offset by the accelerated amount of tax-deductible expense and by the recovery of salvage value, thereby resulting in a lower overall cost under the capital lease.

Lease versus Purchase of Automobile

One approach to gaining lower monthly payments is to lease rather than purchase an automobile. Incentives offered in the late 1980s by major U.S. auto manufacturers have made leasing attractive to individuals wanting new cars without high monthly loan payments.

To illustrate the application of present value analysis to leasing, consider that an individual has a choice of acquiring a $15,000 automobile by either purchasing it using thirty-six-month, 12 percent financing or signing a thirty-six-month lease with a guaranteed residual value of $5,000. In both cases the buyer or lessee must pay insurance and taxes and make a $3,000 down payment. The monthly payment under the purchase arrangement is $399 (see Table 5.3).

The monthly payment under the lease arrangement depends on the dealer's competitiveness. Assume that the dealer structures the lease so that the monthly lease payments and residual value discounted at the 12 percent market rate of interest, plus the down payment, equal the usual selling price of the automobile plus 15 percent. In this case the total would have to be $15,000 plus $2,250 ($15,000 x 15%), or $17,250. The equation required to determine the lease payments is $X $P36/1$ + $5,000 $p36/1$ + $3,000 = PV = $17,250, where X is the lease payment, $P36/1$ is the factor for thirty-six periods at the 1 percent monthly interest rate, $5,000 is the residual value guaranteed at the end of the lease term, and $3,000 is the down payment. Substituting the appropriate factors, the equation becomes ($X) (30.108) + ($5,000) (.699) + $3,000 = $17,250, and $X = $357 (rounded).

The loan payment is $42 more per month than the lease payment. Therefore, the lease arrangement satisfies the objective of a lower monthly payment. The lease payment can be further lowered if the automobile dealer accepts a lower rate of return (lower discount rate), a lease markup of less than 15 percent, or some other modification of the terms involved in the monthly lease payment calculation to arrive at a mutually agreeable lease arrangement when negotiating with the lessee.

Does the lower lease payment justify accepting the lease arrangement? The appraised value of the car will either equal the $5,000 residual at the end of the lease term or will be greater or less than $5,000. In all cases the lessee (purchaser) has the opportunity to buy the automobile for the $5,000 guaranteed residual value. Regardless of whether the automobile is purchased, the lessee will give up $5,000 at the end of the lease term. That is, the lease is structured so that the dealer receives $5,000 cash, a car valued at $5,000, or a combination of the car plus cash equaling $5,000 at the end of the lease.

In calculating the $357 monthly lease payment, the dealer allowed for an additional 15 percent markup on the car. Therefore, the present value of the cash flows associated with the lease will be greater than those associated with an outright purchase. Further, if the appraised value is less than the residual value, the buyer will incur additional cost under the lessee arrangement. However, if the appraised value exceeds $5,000, the lessee gains an equity interest and may receive the excess from the dealer. The present value of the excess can be compared to the additional 15 percent ($2,250) markup. If the present value exceeds $2,250, the net cost of the lease arrangement will be less than that of the purchase arrangement.

The excess appraisal value required to make the two arrangements equal in cost can be determined by solving the equation $X\ p36/1 = PV = \$2,250$ where X is the excess amount to be discounted thirty-six periods at the monthly market rate of interest of 1 percent. Substituting the present value of 1 factor, the equation is $(\$X)\ (.699) = \$2,250$, and $X = \$3,219$. Thus, the appraised value of the $15,000 automobile at the end of the three-year period would have to be $8,219 ($5,000 guaranteed amount plus $3,219 excess) for the two alternatives to be of equal cost, an unlikely occurrence.

7

—

Real Estate

REAL ESTATE VALUATION

Like other investments, the value of real estate can be measured in terms of the future cash flows generated. The maximum amount an investor should pay for a real estate investment is the present value of future cash flows associated with real estate. If the present value of a real estate investment's cash flows is $210,000 and a seller is asking $300,000, the property is obviously overvalued. The following example illustrates the calculation of a real estate investment's present value.

Assume a rental property will be held for five years and is expected to generate an after-tax cash flow of $50,000 at the end of each year. The selling price (terminal or reversion value) of the property at the end of the five-year holding period is estimated to be $350,000. The investor desires a 16 percent return for this risk category of real estate. Calculation of the present value is a three-step process:

1. Discount the ordinary annuity of $50,000 for five years at 16 percent.
2. Calculate the present value of the single future sum of $350,000 received five years hence and discounted at 16 percent.
3. Sum the present values calculated in the first two steps.

The equation used to solve this problem follows: present value of the investment = $50,000 $P5/16$ + $350,000 $p5/16$. Substituting the appropriate present value factors, the equation becomes ($50,000) (3.274) + ($350,000) (.476) = value of the real estate = $153,700

+ \$166,600 = \$330,300. The potential investor should not pay more than \$330,300 if a return of 16 percent is desired.

Note that as the risk of the investment rises, the discount rate rises, resulting in a lower value for the real estate. For instance, if a 20 percent return is desired in the example, the present value drops to \$290,250.

LEVEL PAYMENT CALCULATION

A second use of present values is to determine the level or fixed payment required to pay for property under a mortgage contract. In real estate terms, this payment is known as a constant. Payment of the constant throughout the loan will provide a return of principal and interest to the lender. For example, if property is purchased at a negotiated price of \$330,000, the investor must decide how much will be paid down and what amount will be financed. Assuming a \$30,000 down payment, the remaining balance of \$300,000 will have to be financed. The level payment required for a given term (time period) to amortize or pay down the loan must include principal and interest. The interest rate and number of payments per year also have to be determined.

For ease of calculation, it will be assumed that the term of the loan is twenty years, interest is at a 12 percent annual rate, and that a single payment is made at the end of each year. The amount of level payment required to be made annually to pay off the loan can be determined using the general equation for the present value of an ordinary annuity. In this case, the equation is $X\,P20/12 = PV$, where X is the level payment and PV = \$300,000, the amount financed. Substituting the $P20/12$ factor from the present value of an ordinary annuity table, the equation becomes (X) (7.469) = \$300,000, and X = \$40,166 = the level annual payment. When the total loan is paid off, the aggregate sum paid will amount to \$803,320 (\$50,166 x 20 payments), of which \$300,000 will be principal and \$503,320 will be interest.

If payments are made semiannually in the example, the general equation has to be adjusted to reflect the greater number of payments and the fraction of the annual interest rate on the loan. The total number of payments would increase to forty (20 years x two payments per year), and the interest rate would drop to 6 percent (12% annual rate ÷ 2). The equation for calculating the level payment would then become: $X\,P40/6 = PV$ = \$300,000. Substituting the $P40/6$ factor, the equation becomes (X) (15.046) = \$300,000, and X = \$19,939. The aggregate sum paid would then be \$797,560 (\$19,939 x 40 payments), of which \$300,000 is principal and \$497,560 is interest.

The total interest cost is reduced by increasing the frequency of the payments. A financial calculator can be used to determine the level monthly payment on this loan and any further savings. The monthly payment required to amortize $300,000 in 240 payments (20 years x 12 payments per year) at a 12 percent annual (1 percent monthly) interest rate is $3,303.26. Multiplying this level monthly payment by 240 produces a total sum paid of $792,782. Therefore, paying monthly instead of semiannually saves approximately $4,778 ($497,560 − $492,782). Obviously paying the loan off in fifteen years instead of twenty years will save further interest dollars.

LOAN BALANCE DETERMINATION

At any time during the term of a loan, the borrower may want to know the amount of the unpaid balance. For example, if a borrower wants to refinance a loan at the end of the fifth year, a present value calculation can be used to determine the unpaid principal balance that must be financed under the new and, it is hoped, more favorable interest rate. Then a fourth application of present value analysis — that of determining whether to refinance — can be made.

To demonstrate, assume the borrower made five annual payments on the $300,000 loan illustrated in the preceding section of the chapter. Calculation of the principal balance owed at any time requires knowledge of the interest rate, the number and frequency of remaining payments, and the level of payment required to amortize (pay off) the loan. Assume further that the loan is being amortized with annual payments at the constant or level payment amount of $40,166 calculated using a 12 percent interest rate. The present value of the remaining fifteen annual payments can then be computed using the equation $40,166 $P15/12 = PV$ = unpaid principal balance. Substituting the $P15/12$ factor from the present value of an ordinary annuity table, the equation becomes ($40,166) (6.811) = PV = unpaid principal balance = $273,571. Note that this payment of $40,166 includes effective interest of 12 percent. Discounting remaining payments at that rate eliminates the interest and results in a present value equal to the total principal still owed.

If the loan was being paid off with semiannual payments of $19,939, then at the end of the fifth year, there would be thirty payments remaining to be discounted at the semiannual interest rate of 6 percent. The general equation of $X Pn/i would still be used, but the numbers would become $19,939 $P30/6 = PV$ = principal balance. Substituting the present value factor, the equation is ($19,939) (13.765) = unpaid principal balance

= $274,460. If monthly payments had been made for the first five years, the sum still owed is $275,233. Note that while more frequent payments reduce the total dollar amounts and interest paid each year, the unpaid principal balances at any point in time are higher.

LOAN REFINANCING

Information on how to calculate level or constant payments to amortize a loan and how to determine the loan balance can be used to determine whether to refinance a loan when interest rates in the market decline. The refinancing decision is based on a calculation of the present value savings resulting from the lower potential interest costs. Additional expenses, such as prepayment penalties on the old loan, origination fees, and legal and other costs associated with refinancing, must be considered. If interest savings from refinancing exceed the additional costs, the loan should be refinanced. The following example outlines the steps in the decision process.

Refer to the loan of $300,000 discussed previously in this chapter. The loan was established at 12 percent annual interest, with level payments to be made in twenty equal annual installments. After five years, the first five installments have been paid, leaving fifteen installments still due. Assume interest rates in the market have dropped to 10 percent. A new loan can be obtained for the unpaid principal balance at 10 percent interest with annual installment payments required for fifteen years. Assume the borrower intends to hold the property only five more years and then sell it. In this case, the time horizon for recognizing benefits on the refinancing is five years. Assume that the following dates apply to this example:

> 1985: original loan obtained
> 1990: date of potential refinancing
> 1995: date borrower intends to sell the property
> 2005: maturity date of either the original loan or new loan

If the original loan was taken out at the beginning of 1985 and annual installments were paid for five years, the refinancing would take place at the beginning of 1990. Since the property will be sold at the beginning of 1995, the benefits of refinancing cover only the period between 1990 and 1995.

Additional facts to consider in this case are that there is a 1 percent prepayment penalty on the old loan, an origination fee of 2 percent on the new loan, and legal and other costs of refinancing totaling approximately $2,000. The first step in determining whether to refinance requires calculating the level payment on the original loan of $300,000. Using 12 percent annual interest and repayment in twenty annual installments, the level payment, calculated previously, is $40,166.

Second, compute the balance of the original loan remaining to be refinanced at the beginning of 1990 after the fifth annual installment. The balance has been determined to be the present value of the remaining fifteen installments discounted at 12 percent, or $273,571.

The third step requires determining the annual level payments necessary to amortize the remaining balance, $273,571, over the next fifteen years at the market interest rate of 10 percent. The level payment is calculated using the general equation for the present value of an ordinary annuity, as follows: $\$X\ P15/10 = PV =$ amount refinanced. Substituting the $P15/10$ factor, the equation becomes $(\$X)\ (7.606) = \$273,571$, and $\$X$ (the level payment) equals $35,968.

Next, the difference between annual payments on the original loan (first step) and on the new loan (third step) is computed. The difference is $40,166 - $35,968 = $4,198, and represents a savings each year if the new loan at 10 percent interest is taken out. Technically, the after-tax savings in annual payments should be calculated. The $4,198 annual savings in payments is attributable to lower interest cost, thereby reducing the amount of interest deductible for tax purposes each year. Assuming a 30 percent tax bracket and full deductibility of interest, the average tax savings lost each year is $1,259 (.30 x $4,198). The net savings from refinancing is therefore $2,939 ($4,198 - $1,259). If after-tax savings are used in the analysis, they should be discounted at an after-tax rate. Normally taxes are ignored in computing the savings and in discounting them.

In the fifth step, the present value of the annuity of savings for the term the property will be held is calculated using the market rate of interest now in effect. In this case, the property will continue to be held for the five-year period 1990 to the beginning of 1995. Ignoring taxes, the present value of the annual savings, calculated in step 4, will equal $4,198 $P5/10 = PV = ($4,198) (3.197, the $P5/10$ factor) = $15,915. (Note that by discounting the after-tax savings of $2,939 by the after-tax rate of 7 percent, $PV = $5,838.)

The sum of all additional expenses (costs) incurred because of the refinancing should now be calculated. (In the chapter on capital budgeting, this type of cost was added to the net investment.) The costs in this case include a prepayment penalty if the original loan is paid off before its term, an origination fee on the new loan, plus legal and other costs. The prepayment penalty equals 1 percent times the loan balance after the fifth installment is paid = (.01) ($273,571) = $2,736. The origination fee was given as 2 percent and is based on the new loan, as follows: (.02) ($273,571) = $5,471. Legal and other costs of refinancing were estimated to be $2,000. The total of these three expenses equals $10,207 ($2,736 + $5,471 + $2,000). (The after-tax cost should be calculated if the after-tax cash savings and discount rate are used in step 5.)

In the final step, the present value of the savings created by the refinancing is compared to the present value of expenses incurred to effect the refinancing. If the savings exceed the expenses, the borrower should refinance. The present value of the savings in this case amounted to $15,915 (step 5), and the present value of the expenses totaled $10,207 (step 6). The net benefit of refinancing in this situation is $5,708 ($15,915 − $10,207). The borrower should refinance.

Additional refinements, including full consideration of the effects of income taxes, can be made to this refinancing example. Prepayment penalties are generally tax deductible when paid, and origination fees can be amortized for tax purposes. Other expenses, such as legal fees, can be considered in calculating the tax basis of property. All of these adjustments tend to reduce the amount of expenses associated with refinancing. Thus, if the refinancing decision is positive without these adjustments, with the adjustments, it will be more beneficial.

Another element that has not been considered is whether under the new loan there would be some loss of equity buildup because of lower payments under the new loan. Equity builds up more rapidly under the new loan because the reduction in annual interest is greater than the reduction in annual payments. The gain in equity buildup under the new loan can be discounted to its present value and added to the benefit of refinancing.

Following the seven steps shown is usually sufficient to arrive at an accurate basis for the refinancing decision. Readers are advised to give recognition to income taxes in the process if the present value of the net benefit or net cost results in marginal values. Reference should also be made to Chapter 5 dealing with bond refundings. Many of the principles illustrated there apply to the refinancing decision.

BALLOON PAYMENT ACCUMULATION

Another present value application is that of determining the fixed amount that must be set aside periodically to make a future lump sum or balloon payment. Sometimes real estate loans require payment of only interest during the term of the loan, with the total principal payable at the end of the loan term in the form of a lump sum or balloon payment. A future value calculation is required to determine the amount that must be placed in a sinking fund established to accumulate the necessary money to make the balloon payment. The amount depends on the frequency of deposits to the fund, the expected return on fund investments, and the total amount to be accumulated to satisfy the lump sum or balloon payment requirement. Consider the following example.

Assume that $50,000 must be accumulated to make a balloon payment five years hence and that funds set aside annually can earn 8 percent. Deposits are to be made to a sinking fund annually at the end of the year. Using the general equation for computing the future value of an ordinary annuity, in this case the equation is $X A5/8 = FV$ = balloon payment = $50,000, where X is the required annual deposit. Substituting the $A5/8$ factor for the future value of an ordinary annuity, the equation becomes (X) (5.867) = $50,000 and $X = $8,522. Assuming the $8,522 deposited at the end of each year for five years earns an 8 percent interest return as planned, the needed $50,000 will be available at the end of the fifth year. Note that the deposits total $42,610 (5 x $8,522). The remainder of the $50,000 requirement is accumulated in the form of interest.

If deposits to the sinking fund can be made quarterly, the equation would become $X A20/2 = FV = $50,000. The $A20/2$ factor represents twenty three-month periods (5 years x 4 quarters per year), and 2 percent quarterly interest (8% annual rate ÷ 4). Substituting the $A20/2$ factor, the equation is (X) (24.297) = $FV = $50,000, and $X,$ the quarterly deposit, is $2,058. The total amount deposited will be $41,160 (20 x $4,058). Because of quarterly compounding of interest, the total deposits are $1,450 ($42,610 – $41,160) less than those made on an annual basis.

Using a financial calculator (because the required table factors are not available in this book), it can be determined that if deposits are made monthly in the example, the $50,000 balloon payment can be accumulated by setting aside $680.49 each period, or $40,829 (60 months x $680.49) total. Even more of the $50,000 balloon payment requirement in this case is accumulated in the form of interest.

The same process can be used in other ways — for example, to save to buy a new roof five years hence at a cost of $50,000 or to determine the size of periodic deposits to set aside at a given return to provide for a child's college education in the future.

LOAN REPAYMENT PERIOD SELECTION

In periods of high interest rates, it may be desirable to finance the acquisition of real estate with a fifteen-year loan rather than with a longer-term loan because the former will result in a much lower total cost. The difference in principal and interest payments can be calculated using present value analysis. Consider the following example.

A decision must be made whether to borrow $80,000 at 10 percent interest on a thirty-year mortgage or on a twenty-year mortgage. Present value calculations can be used to determine periodic mortgage payments under both alternatives and to help determine the amount of savings under the shorter loan period.

The level payment calculation on the thirty-year mortgage, assuming annual payments, is X $P30/10 = PV$ = amount financed = $80,000. Substituting the $P30/10$ factor, the equation becomes (X) (9.427) = $80,000, and X, the annual payment, equals $8,486. Following the same approach for the twenty-year mortgage, the factor is 8.514 and the annual payment is $9,396, only $910 ($9,396 − $8,486) greater than under the thirty-year mortgage. The cash flow available to the purchaser may determine which loan will be more desirable. However, note that on a monthly loan schedule, the difference in payments for the two alternatives is only $70.

The total costs on each mortgage can be readily determined from the annual payments. The sum of the annuity of payments to be made on the thirty-year loan is $254,580 ($8,486 × 30 annual payments). The total amount payable under the twenty-year loan equals $187,920 ($9,396 × 20 annual payments). By choosing the twenty-year repayment period, the borrower can save $66,660 ($254,580 − $187,920) in interest. Not only is the mortgage paid off in ten fewer years, but the cost of doing so ($910 × 20 annual payments, or $18,200) is much less than the $66,660 interest saved. Even more dramatic examples can be provided using higher interest rates. If interest rates rise to 12 percent, the difference in annual payments on an $80,000 mortgage is only $779, or $58 per month, under a twenty-year versus thirty-year term.

Home buyers requiring $80,000 financing at 10 percent interest, with monthly payments over thirty years, are surprised to find out that the home will have a total cost to them of $252,741, more than triple the amount financed. This highlights the importance of the decision about the mortgage term (twenty versus thirty years) and the rate of interest. If the interest rate on the mortgage is 9.5 percent instead of 10 percent, the total amount paid will be $242,166, and a savings of $10,575 will result.

Thus, even a small annual interest saving over the loan period provides a significant benefit.

ADJUSTABLE VERSUS FIXED RATE MORTGAGES

From 1963 to early 1989 interest rates for mortgages have risen from approximately 5.5 percent to 10.5 percent. During that period, rates went as high as 14.7 percent and as low as 5.2 percent. To accommodate these changing interest rates, financial institutions developed adjustable rate mortgages (ARM). Now a potential purchaser can choose between a fixed rate mortgage, on which the interest rate remains constant for the entire term of the loan, or an ARM, on which the interest rate is changed periodically according to a specified interest index. Total interest rate changes on the adjustable mortgages may have an annual cap, for example, a 1 percent rate increase per year, and a maximum cap, for example, 5 percent, during the term of the loan. Present value analysis can be used to compare an adjustable rate mortgage with a fixed rate mortgage to determine which, if either, is more desirable. Prediction of future interest rates is not easy, but some analysis of potential future rate changes is necessary so purchasers can make an informed judgment.

The purchaser's dilemma in our example is whether to choose a fixed rate mortgage at 10 percent or an 8 percent ARM. A comparison of the total cost for both loans is required. The obvious problem is forecasting interest rates for the twenty- or thirty-year term to determine which is the better mortgage. Generally it might be concluded that since individuals, businesses, and governments are taking on more debt, future interest rates will tend to rise. But by how much?

To illustrate the present value analysis required, we will assume that a thirty-year fixed rate mortgage of $80,000 can be obtained at a 10 percent interest rate, while an ARM will initially have an 8 percent rate. Further, we will assume that future rates will rise by 2 percent in Year 10 of the mortgage and by another 2 percent in Year 20. (The normal assumption is that interest rates increase gradually in smaller increments, such as from 8 percent to 9 percent, then to 10 percent, and so on. However, periodic increases of two percentage points are assumed to simplify computations.)

Assume an ARM is obtained at the beginning of 1989 at an 8 percent rate, that the adjustable rate is expected to rise at the beginning of 1999 to 10 percent, and again in 2009 to 12 percent. The thirty-year loan term will extend to the end of 2018. Its fixed rate will remain constant at 10 percent throughout the thirty-year loan term. To determine which is the better loan — that is, the one with the least cost under the assumptions made — requires a number of calculations.

First, the total cost of the fixed rate mortgage is determined. Annual payments will be used in this analysis since the present value tables cannot accommodate 360 monthly payments (monthly payments can be readily computed with a financial calculator). The total cost of the fixed rate loan will be the annual level payment multiplied by thirty years. The level payment is determined using the general equation for the present value of an ordinary annuity, as follows: X $P30/10 = PV =$ amount financed $= \$80,000$. Substituting the $P30/10$ factor, the equation becomes $(\$X)$ $(9.427) = \$80,000$, and $\$X = \$8,486$, the level payment, which includes principal and interest. The total cost of the fixed rate loan is $\$254,580$ ($\$8,486 \times 30$).

Second, the total cost of the ARM for the first ten years is calculated. The level payment required at 8 percent interest is computed under the assumption that the interest rate will not change during the thirty-year loan period. Therefore the level payment can be calculated as before using the equation $\$X$ $P30/8 = \$80,000$. Substituting the $P30/8$ factor, the equation is $(\$X)$ $(11.258) = \$80,000$ and $\$X = \$7,106$. If ten annual payments of this amount are made before the interest rate changes, the total cost for the segment 1989–1998 (the first ten years) will be $\$71,060$ ($\$7,106 \times 10$).

The next step is to compute the loan balance on the ARM at the end of 1998. Interest rates will rise to 10 percent at the beginning of 1998, and a new level payment will have to be calculated. The 1998 year-end balance should equal the present value of the twenty remaining payments of $\$7,106$. The present value of an annuity equation in this case is $\$7,106$ $P20/8 = PV = (\$7,106)$ $(9.818) = \$69,767$, the balance remaining on the ARM. A new level payment must be calculated for this amount of financing to reflect the rise in the interest rate to 10 percent. Therefore, solving the equation, $\$X$ $P20/10 = \$69,767$. By substituting the $P20/10$ factor of 8.514, the level payment equals $\$X = \$8,194$. Assuming ten annual payments are made before interest rates change again, the total cost of the ARM from 1999 to 2008 will amount to $\$81,940$ ($\$8,194 \times 10$ years).

Steps 5 and 6 are a repeat of steps 3 and 4 but for the last ten years. The loan balance in the ARM at the end of year 2008 has to be calculated. As in step 3 the loan balance equals the present value of the remaining payments discounted at the rate in effect before the rate change. In this case the equation is $\$8,194$ $P10/10 = PV =$ remaining loan balance, where $P10/10$ is the factor for the last ten years of the loan at 10 percent interest. The equation becomes ($8,194) (6.145) = $50,352, the loan balance when the interest on the ARM rises to 12 percent. This amount must be amortized with a new level payment required using the 12 percent rate for the last ten years of the ARM (year 2009–year 2018) on the loan balance of $50,352. The equation needed is X $P10/12$ - $50,352. Substituting the $P10/12$ factor, the equation becomes (X) (5.650) = $50,352, and $X = $8,912. When these last ten payments are made between year 20 and the maturity date of the loan, the total payments equal $89,120 ($8,192 x 10).

The sum of the payments made on the ARM during the three ten-year segments can now be calculated as step 7. The total payment for the three time segments amounts to $71,060 [1989–1998] + $81,940 [1999–2008] + $89,120 [2009–2018] = $242,120, the total cost of the ARM. Step 8 requires that the total cost of the fixed rate mortgage ($254,580) be compared with the total cost of the ARM ($242,120). Thus, the ARM is cheaper than the fixed rate mortgage by the amount of $12,460 ($254,580 – $242,120). However, further analysis may be necessary.

Note that the $12,460 cost advantage associated with the ARM is based on the absolute dollar payments made over thirty years. The cash flows can be adjusted for the tax shield (tax savings) provided by interest. The ATCF for both the fixed rate and ARM can then be discounted to their present value at time zero, the date financing is obtained. Normally the difference in present value amounts will support the same decision reached using absolute dollar amounts. Therefore, the latter may normally be used. However, if interest rates under the ARM are expected to rise significantly in the very early years of the mortgage period, present value calculation may support a decision different from that using absolute dollar amounts.

A relatively easy approach to the present value question is to compute the rate implicit in the projected ARM payments. The present value equation should be set equal to the dollar amount financed — in this case, $80,000. The calculated implicit rate on the ARM can be compared to the fixed rate to determine which alternative is better. Another approach is to discount the projected ARM payments to their present value using the fixed rate. If the present value is less than the amount mortgaged, the ARM should be selected. In this case the present value of the ARM payments discounted at 10 percent if $71,215, calculated using the following equation: $7,106$ $P10/10$ + ($8,194) ($P20/10 – P10/10$) + ($8,912) ($P30/10 – P20/10$).

The example illustrates the process used when a comparison is to be made between a fixed rate mortgage and an ARM. Although the example was simplified to make calculations easier, the steps outlined are the same even with more complicated data. Every time rates change, a new mortgage balance and a new level payment have to be calculated. Frequent changes could result in twenty-five segments to the loan instead of three as shown in the example. Other complications might include monthly payment calculations and decreases and increases in interest rates. Use of reasonable and realistic assumptions improves the decision process.

8

Business Fund Accumulations

Businesses accumulate funds for a variety of purposes — retirement of bonds and plant expansion projects, among others. Most cases covered in prior chapters required present value computations; fund accumulation cases require calculation of future values. This chapter covers general principles applicable to fund accumulations, with special emphasis on pension plans.

GENERAL PRINCIPLES

Fund accumulation cases normally require determination of periodic deposits to an interest-bearing account so that a specific amount of money is available at a future date for a specific purpose. Deposits might also be invested in stocks or mutual funds where the annual earnings rate has to be estimated using historical and other data. In some cases the amount to be accumulated is given; in other cases it must first be determined. For example, a corporation planning to retire bonds with a maturity value of $100,000 must accumulate that amount before the bonds mature. On the other hand, if an individual plans to have an annual retirement income of $10,000 for fifteen years following retirement, the present value at retirement of that annuity must be calculated before periodic fund accumulation deposits are computed. Other cases involving fund accumulations may simply require determining the future value of a given series of periodic deposits to a fund, assuming a certain compound growth rate.

Examples presented in the chapter illustrate calculations of periodic deposits under a variety of circumstances. After determining the amount to be accumulated, it is necessary to identify the period of time over which the fund is to be accumulated, the timing and frequency of periodic deposits, the expected rate of earnings on amounts deposited, and whether the earnings are subject to state or federal income tax.

Frequency of Deposits

The frequency of deposits may be established by contract, such as in a bond indenture, or it may be set to meet the cash flow pattern of the organization or individual in question. Usual practice is to defer deposits to the end of each period to allow time to earn the amount to be deposited. If deposits are made frequently — for example, quarterly rather than annually — then a higher proportion of the amount accumulated will be represented by earnings, reflecting the effects of more frequent compounding of earnings; absolute dollar amounts of periodic deposits required will be lower as a consequence.

Interest Rates

The interest rate to use in calculating fund earnings must normally be estimated unless the funding period is quite short and deposits are made to passbook saving or other accounts that have firmly established fixed rates of return. Some investments, including time certificates of deposit and zero coupon bonds, with maturity dates ranging from several months to several years can also negate the need for estimating interest rates. Specific rates assumed when making future value calculations should reflect earnings available on the types of investments allowed or planned with fund deposits.

As the number of fund accumulation periods increases, it becomes increasingly difficult to predict accurately the earnings rate to use, especially if deposits will be applied to a variety of investments. One technique for dealing with this uncertainty is to use a minimal rate that is virtually guaranteed, with any excess earnings to be withdrawn from the fund for other uses. Another approach is to adjust the deposits periodically to reflect new earnings rates and fund accumulation balances to date. For example, the balance at the end of five years of a twenty-year fund accumulation, plus interest on that balance at the revised earnings rate projected for the remaining fifteen years, can be deducted from the required balance at maturity to determine the future amount remaining to be accumulated. Amounts of future deposits to be made in Years 6–20 can be recalculated to reflect earnings rates projected after Year 5.

Taxability of Earnings

The final variable to consider in planning fund accumulations is taxability of earnings. Earnings on some investments, such as municipal bonds, may be exempt from federal income tax; earnings on most other investments are not. Special care should be exercised in determining the taxability of earnings on funds accumulated by individuals. Federal, state, and sometimes local income taxes may apply to earnings. The question of state tax laws may be especially critical for individuals who move to other states and transfer funds to accounts in those states. Potential penalties for account withdrawals must also be considered. Once income tax rates applicable to fund earnings are determined, an after-tax earnings rate can be used to calculate required periodic fund deposits. For example, if fund earnings are 10 percent and combined federal and state tax rates total 40 percent, then the after-tax rate of 6 percent (10 percent earnings less 40 percent lost to taxes) should be used in determining periodic fund deposits.

FUND ACCUMULATION PRINCIPLES ILLUSTRATED

After the variables entering into the calculation of fund requirements are known, the amount of periodic deposits can be determined using the general equation for computing the future value of an ordinary annuity.

Required Periodic Deposits for Given Future Value

Assume $100,000 is to be accumulated in a fund requiring equal deposits at the end of each year for ten years, with annual after-tax earnings of 4 percent. The following time line represents the cash flow pattern:

```
/-----/-----/-----/--- ...  --/-----/
 0     1     2     3    ...   9     10
       $X    $X    $X   ...   $X    $X
----------------------------------->  FV
```

The required annual deposit is calculated by solving the equation $X A10/4 = FV = $100,000, where $X is the annual deposit and A10/4 is the year 10, 4 percent factor for the future value of an ordinary annuity.

Substituting the $A10/4$ factor, the equation becomes (X) (12.006) = $100,000; $X = $8,329. Principal deposits for the ten years equal $83,290 (10 years x $8,329), with the remaining $16,710 portion of the $100,000 fund accumulated through earnings.

If deposits had been made quarterly in the example, $18,160 would have been provided by earnings, calculated as follows: $X A40/1 = FV = $100,000, where $A40/1$ represents forty quarterly periods at a 1 percent quarterly earnings rate. Substituting the $A40/1$ factor, the equation becomes (X) (48.886) = $100,000; $X = $2,046, and total principal deposits equal $81,840 (40 deposits x $2,046). Monthly deposits and compounding would result in an even higher portion of the $100,000 being provided by earnings.

Effect of Changing Interest Rate on Accumulations

Had the after-tax annual earnings rate in the example risen to 5 percent after Year 4, amounts deposited during the last six years could be recalculated (assume initial annual deposits as in the original example). The following time line illustrates the cash flow pattern:

```
/------/------/------/------/------/-- ... --/------/
0      1      2      3      4      5   ...   9     10

    $8,329 $8,329 $8,329 $8,329  $X  ...    $X    $X

----------------------------------------------------->  FV
```

Solving the equation $8,329 $A4/4 = FV$, the portion of the $100,000 fund accumulated the first four years is determined to be $35,365 ($8,329 x 4.246 [the $A4/4$ factor]). It is then necessary to determine the amount the $35,365 will accumulate to by the end of year 10, assuming after-tax interest at 5 percent the last six years. Using the equation for calculating the future value of a single amount, the $35,365 will accumulate to $47,389, determined as follows: $35,365 $a6/5 = FV$ = ($35,365$) (1.340) = $47,389. Therefore equal periodic deposits, X, made at the end of each of Years 5–10 must provide the remaining $52,611 funding required ($100,000 – $47,389). As depicted in the time line illustration, the remaining deposits constitute an ordinary annuity for six periods and can be calculated by solving the equation $X A6/5 = FV$ = $52,611. Substituting the $A6/5$ factor, the equation becomes (X) (6.802) = $52,611; $X = $7,735. Therefore, the $8,329 annuity of the first four years compounded at 4 percent must be supplemented by an annuity of $7,735 for the last six years, compounded at 5 percent.

SINKING FUND ACCUMULATIONS

Business and other organizations need to accumulate funds for a number of purposes. Two common types of business fund accumulations are sinking funds for bond retirement, plant expansion, or other uses and investment funds for use in satisfying pension obligations. Calculations for determining deposits to sinking funds are straightforward and pose no significant difficulties. Pension fund calculations often require numerous assumptions and subsequent adjustments to reflect new information.

Provisions of a bond issuance may require that during the time that bonds are outstanding a company accumulate sufficient funds to retire the bonds at maturity. Annual contributions to such funds, referred to as *bond sinking funds,* are calculated as illustrated in the following example. Assume ten-year term bonds with a maturity value of $100,000, after-tax interest earnings of 6 percent, and a provision for sinking fund contributions at the end of each year until maturity. The time line depicting the contributions follows:

```
/-----/-----/-----/----  ...  ----/
0     1     2     3     ...    10

      $X    $X    $X    ...    $X
------------------------------> FV = $100,000
```

The annual contribution, X, can be determined using the general equation for calculating the future value of an ordinary annuity, where FV = $100,000 = $X\ A\ 10/6$ = (X) (13.181); X = $7,587. Annual contributions are made at the end of each period. If they were made at the beginning of each period, they would be determined using the equation for an annuity due. Similar calculations apply to the determination of amounts to be contributed to sinking funds established for plant expansion or other purposes.

PENSION FUNDING

Many employers must make periodic contributions to a pension fund for employees. Many pension programs are characterized by high proportions of company employees who are eligible for pension benefits. Higher dollar benefits and longer benefit periods have contributed to the growth in employers' pension obligations. An understanding of pension obligations requires that the interrelationships existing among the time value of money, future dollar benefits to be paid, inflation, mortality rates, and other pension-related variables be considered. Further, the distinction between defined benefit and defined contribution plans must be understood.

Pension-related present value calculations can become highly complex in practice. Therefore the following information should be supplemented with the services of qualified actuaries and pension plan specialists when making pension decisions involving large dollar amounts or large numbers of employees.

Defined Benefit versus Defined Contribution Pension Plans

Under a *defined benefit plan,* employee pension benefits are fixed relative to a benefit formula, and the employer's periodic contributions to the pension fund have to be sufficient to cover those benefits. Benefits are normally a function of average wage or salary figures, years of service, and other factors that at the time of pension funding can usually only be estimated. For example, the retirement benefit might be defined as 3 percent of an employee's highest annual wage for each year of service up to twenty-five years. An employer's annual contributions to a pension fund must take into consideration employee turnover rates, expected pension fund earnings, and other factors that are also based on estimates. Thus, annual pension fund contributions may have to be revised periodically to reflect changes in estimates, including retroactive funding adjustments, creating an element of uncertainty for employers.

To reduce the level of risk concerning required dollar contributions to pension plans, employers can offer *defined contribution plans.* They are more manageable than defined benefit plans because there is no uncertainty regarding dollar amounts of pension contributions required each year. The employer's and, if the plan is contributory, the employee's contributions are fixed, normally at a percentage of wages or profits, the latter if tied to a profit-sharing plan. For example, the employer contributes to a pension plan an amount equal to 6 percent of each employee's annual wage or salary. Pension benefits therefore become a function of the amount that annual contributions to the pension plan accumulate to prior to an employee's retirement and how long the employee is to receive benefits after retirement. Once having made periodic contributions, the employer has no further obligation, a feature that makes such plans attractive. However, employers should compare costs associated with each of the two types of pension plans for their respective organizations before concluding that one type of plan is better.

Variables Influencing Pension Costs

A number of factors enter into the calculation of pension costs: qualifying employees, employee turnover rates, assumed interest earnings on amounts funded (pension fund earnings), employee compensation levels, employee retirement ages, employee mortality ages, and years of required service before pension benefits vest (that is, remain with an employee regardless of continued employment). Employee turnover rates are calculated to reflect the portion of employees whose benefits will vest. The rate of interest earned on pension fund deposits directly influences an employer's annual pension fund contribution; high interest rates reduce funding requirements. Employee retirement ages compared to current ages dictate the time periods over which pension fund contributions should be made. Mortality tables reflect the probable number of years employees will receive pension benefits upon retirement.

Calculating Pension Fund Contributions

The amount of pension plan funding required of an employer under a defined benefit plan is the present value of all future benefits to be paid to employees as a result of their current year's services. For example, if as a result of this year's service an employee earns the right to receive $50 per month for life after retirement, then the employer's current funding requirement is the present value at retirement of the $50 monthly benefit for the number of years the employee is expected to live, discounted from retirement to the current year; that is, the cost is the present value of the deferred annuity earned by the employee.

Under a defined contribution plan, required periodic deposits are based on the contribution formula — for example, a percentage of wages. The discount rate to be used in making the present value calculations is the expected earnings rate on any pension fund contributions, including balances available after retirement but not yet distributed. The calculation is repeated for each additional year of service rendered by the employee. From the viewpoint of a company as a whole, however, periodic deposits must be adjusted to reflect employee turnover rates and the actual funding period chosen by the employer. Further adjustments are required for changes in interest rates, mortality table factors, and other variables integral to the calculation of pension benefits, costs, or deposits under the two types of pension plans.

Assume that instead of earning fixed monthly retirement benefits, employees with sufficient years of service earn an annual benefit equal to 80 percent of the average annual wage of their last five years of employment with the company before retirement. Again the company's funding requirement is equal to the present value of the benefits to be paid. However, instead of being fixed at, for example, $50 per month for each year of service, the benefit is based on a future wage rate that must necessarily be estimated.

Estimating Future Wages

One way to estimate future wages is to determine the average annual compound growth rate in a company's wage structure and to apply that rate to each employee's current wage. For example, assume that the average wage paid ten years ago by the company was $10,000 and is now $14,800. Using the general equation for calculating the future value of 1, the ten-year compound growth rate in wages = $10,000 $a10/i = FV$ = $14,800. Solving the equation, the $a10/i$ factor is 1.480 and is found on the period 10 line of the "Present Value of $1" table under the 4 percent column. Hence, wages increase an average of 4 percent per year.

If a current employee has an annual wage of $12,000 and will work eighteen more years before retiring, then his or her expected wage thirteen years hence (five years before retirement) will be $19,980 ($12,000 $a13/4 = FV$ = $12,000 x 1.665), and the wage eighteen years hence will be $24,312 ($12,000 $a18/4 = FV$ = $12,000 x 2.026). Basing the average wage for the last five years on the two projected wage figures, the average is $22,146 ([.5 x $19,980] + $24,312). Multiplying $22,146 by 80 percent gives a defined annual benefit of $17,717. An employer must decide whether the cost of funding this defined benefit is greater than the costs associated with a defined contribution plan.

Defined Benefit versus Defined Contribution Plan: An Example

Assume an employer is trying to decide which of two pension benefit options to offer an individual employee. Under the first option, the employee receives an annual retirement benefit equal to 50 percent of her average annual wage for the last five years preceding retirement. Assume the employer will fund the pension plan by making equal annual deposits to the pension fund over the employee's remaining twenty years of service. Assume further that the benefit will be $20,000 (calculated as illustrated in the example in the preceding section). Life expectancy tables indicate that the employee will live twelve years beyond retirement. Any undistributed pension fund deposits will earn 6 percent interest.

Under the second option, the employee receives an annual benefit based on the amount available in a pension fund into which the employer contributes at the end of each year of service an amount equal to 10 percent of that year's wage. For the sake of illustration, it is assumed that the employee's average annual wage for the last twenty years of service is $34,000 and that the employer contributes 10 percent of that amount to the pension fund at the end of each year. The employer's cost under the second option is readily computed to be $3,400 annually ($34,000 x 10 percent). The first option requires that the present value of the defined pension benefit of $20,000 be calculated, followed by a calculation of the annual contribution necessary to fund the benefit. The following time line illustrates the cash flows associated with the plan:

```
/-------/-------/-------/--...--/-------/--...--/
 0       1       2       3 ... 20      21  ... 32
Start                           Retire          End

                                $20,000 ... $20,000

                                PV <--------------

        $X      $X      $X ... $X
-----------------------------> FV
```

The employee enters the plan at time zero and retires at the end of Year 20. Retirement benefits will be paid to the employee at the end of Years 21–32, the twelve-year retirement period. The present value at the end of Year 20 of the twelve-year, $20,000 retirement annuity is the amount that must be accumulated during the twenty-year period the employee works prior to retirement. The amount that must be contributed to the retirement fund by the employer at the end of each of the twenty years is indicated by $X.

Given the 6 percent interest rate that the undistributed pension fund balance earns, the present value of the pension benefit payments can be calculated using the general equation for the present value of an annuity, as follows: $PV = \$20,000 \ P12/6 = (\$20,000) \ (8.384) = \$167,680$. The amount of equal annual deposits the employer must contribute to the pension fund to meet the $167,680 requirement is calculated using the general equation for the future value of an annuity. The equation is X $A20/6 = FV = \$167,680 = (\$X) (36.786); \$X = \$4,558 =$ required annual contribution by the employer.

The employer's annual contribution will be greater by $1,158 ($4,558 – $3,400) under the defined benefit option. Therefore, from the employer's viewpoint the defined contribution plan should be chosen. Note, however, that the decision is sensitive to interest rate changes. Assuming 8 percent interest earnings, the calculations under the first option become $PV = \$20,000 \ P12/8 = (\$20,000) (7.536) =$ required fund accumulation = $150,720. The annual contribution to be made by the employer then becomes $FV = \$150,720 = \$X \ A20/8 = (\$X) (45.762); \$X = \$3,294$. In this case the defined benefit plan is less costly than the defined contribution plan by $106 ($3,294 versus $3,400) per year.

Employers who offer defined benefit plans can take advantage of high interest rates to reduce the cost of meeting future obligations to employees. In some cases pension funding patterns and pension investments are established when assumed earnings rates are relatively low. If interest rates rise and reduce funding requirements, employers can lock into the high rates by purchasing from insurance companies and other institutions annuity contracts that satisfy the employer's pension obligations to employees. Often the amounts funded by employers prior to the purchase of an annuity contract exceed the cost of the annuities because funding was based on a lower assumed rate of return.

9

Personal Fund Accumulations

Individuals have historically established savings and other accounts for use in funding retirement needs, for funding their children's educations, and for other purposes. Future value calculations are useful in determining required periodic deposits to such funds. This chapter presents a variety of fund accumulation examples, including use of state education bonds and supplementary retirement accounts and the adjustments for effects of inflation, income taxes, and other factors on fund accumulations.

Generally periodic fund contributions for individuals are calculated in the same manner as for a bond sinking fund. However, bond sinking fund contributions are contractual in nature and are relatively fixed depending on actual versus planned fund earnings. Personal fund accumulations are much more flexible in terms of the timing and amounts of periodic deposits, investment of funds, sheltering of earnings from current income taxes, and future amounts to be accumulated. Further, personal fund accumulations are often contingent on assumed needs, considering effects of inflation and related factors. Income taxes are considered separately in the next example, followed by illustrations of various fund accumulation cases that incorporate adjustments for effects of income taxes, inflation, and other variables.

EFFECTS OF INCOME TAXES

Adjustments for the effects of income taxes on fund accumulations can be made by calculating future values using an after-tax rate of return. If the tax rates and income levels of individuals who are accumulating funds remain constant, no problems arise. However, future income tax rates often vary because of tax law changes or changes in individual income levels. In other cases, income taxes can be deferred or avoided by using tax-sheltered annuities, investing in municipal securities or state education bonds, or other means. Care must be taken to identify taxable earnings and to measure the effects of changes in income tax laws and rates as accurately as possible and to incorporate these factors into fund accumulation calculations. It is important to consider both state and federal income tax laws, especially if individuals move into new tax jurisdictions and transfer funds from one location to another.

The effects of tax rate changes illustrated here often result in a pattern of unequal cash flows and complicate fund accumulation calculations. For example, assume that an individual plans to accumulate $40,000 over an eight-year period and that annual year-end fund contributions earn 10 percent interest. The individual's average income tax rate is expected to increase from 30 percent to 40 percent after Year 5 because of an increase in personal income. Assuming annual fund contributions of $3,000 the first five years, the following time line illustrates the cash flow pattern for the fund:

```
/-----/-----/-----/-----/-----/-----/-----/-----/
0      1     2     3     4     5     6     7     8

    $3000 $3000 $3000 $3000 $3000  $X    $X    $X

---------------------------------------------->  FV
```

To calculate annual deposits required in Years 6–8, it is first necessary to determine the portion of the $40,000 fund requirement that is satisfied by deposits made the first five years. Using the general equation for calculating the future value of an ordinary annuity, the calculation becomes $3,000 $A5/7 = FV = (\$3,000) (5.751) = \$17,253$, where 7 percent is the after-tax earnings rate for the first five years (10% earnings – 30% tax rate). However, $17,253 is the future value at the end of only Year 5 and must be compounded at the 6 percent after-tax interest rate (10% – 40% lost to taxes) in effect from Year 6 through Year 8 to arrive at the future value at the end of Year 8. Thus, $17,253 $a3/6 = FV$ = (\$17,253) (1.191) = \$20,548$. Therefore, the remaining fund requirement of $19,452 ($40,000 – $20,548) must be met through the last three deposits made at the end of each of Years 6–8. The last three annual deposits of $X are determined as follows: $X $A3/6 = FV = \$19,452$

= (X) (3.184); $X = \$6,109$, where three years is the period covered by the ordinary annuity after Year 5.

Had earnings in the example been exempt from income tax, the before-tax earnings rate of 10 percent would have been used in calculating required annual deposits, regardless of whether a fixed dollar deposit for the first five years is assumed. Had tax on the earnings simply been deferred until the $40,000 was withdrawn, it would be necessary to accumulate an amount that, after income taxes at the withdrawal date, would provide the required $40,000. For example, assume the equal annual deposits made at the end of each of the eight years earn 10 percent interest. The total interest earned will be taxed at a 40 percent rate when the fund is withdrawn immediately after the last deposit. If earnings are not taxed, the equation for calculating the annual deposits is X $A8/10 = FV = \$40,000 = (\$X) (11.436); X = \$3,498$. If earnings are taxed when the fund is withdrawn at the end of Year 8, then tax of $4,806 (40% tax rate x interest of $12,016, where interest equals $40,000 less the eight deposits of $3,498) must be provided for in addition to the $40,000.

EDUCATION FUNDS

Variables that must be considered when establishing education funds are future cash needs, expected rates of return on invested amounts, the period of time over which to accumulate funds, types of investments to make, and other variables discussed under the heading of general principles of fund accumulation.

The amount to be accumulated is a function of expectations concerning future education costs and amounts of financial aid for which each child may be eligible. Financial aid eligibility can be discussed with a high school or college counselor. Future tuition costs can be estimated using the historical average compound rate of tuition growth for the type of educational institution being considered. That rate can be applied to the current tuition cost for the number of years until the child is to begin an educational program. To understand better various aspects of fund accumulation for education purposes, consider the following cases.

Estimation of Future Tuition Costs

If annual tuition cost ten years ago was $4,000 and is now $7,164, then the average compound annual rate of growth in tuition is 6 percent, computed as follows: $\$4,000$ $a10/i = FV = \$7,164$, where $a10/i$ is the factor for calculating the future value of a single amount compounded at i rate of interest for ten years. Solving the equation, the factor is calculated to be 1.791 and is found under the 6 percent column on the period 10 line. Assuming that tuition will continue to increase at a 6 percent rate until a child enrolls in college fifteen years hence, annual tuition cost at that time can be calculated by solving the following equation for the future value of a single amount: $7,164 $a15/6 = FV = (\$7,164) (2.397) =$ $17,172.

Calculation of Deposits to Education Fund

To simplify calculations, assume that four times the amount determined in the preceding case is to be accumulated by the end of the fifteenth year in a savings account that provides after-tax interest income of 5 percent. Further, assume that interest on any unused balance starting after Year 15 will approximately cover subsequent increases in tuition. The parents plan to make deposits to the account at the end of each year. The amount of the annual deposits can be determined by solving the general equation for the future value of an ordinary annuity, as follows: $\$X A15/5 = FV = \$68,688$ (4 × \$17,172), where $\$X$ is the annual deposit and $A15/5$ is the factor for an ordinary annuity for fifteen years at 5 percent. Substituting the factor, the equation becomes $(\$X) (21.579) =$ $68,688; $\$X = \$3,183$. Thus, the parents must annually contribute \$3,183 to the education fund. Accounts with higher interest earnings, more frequent deposits, or a tax shelter status can be used to reduce the required annual contribution amount.

Assume in the illustration that the parents believe they can afford annual deposits of only \$2,000 the first five years and plan to compensate by making contributions to the education fund in amounts exceeding the originally determined amount of \$3,183 each of the last ten years. The following time line is useful in identifying the cash flows in this situation:

```
/----/----/-- ...--/----/----/----/-- ...--/-----/
0    1    2   ... 5   6    7    8         14   15

$2,000 $2,000...$2,000 $X    $X   $X   ... $X    $X

-----------------------------------------------> FV
```

Assuming the \$68,688 amount to be accumulated and the 5 percent interest rate do not change, then a three-step calculation must be made:

1. The value of the $2,000 ordinary annuity at the end of Year 5 is calculated by solving the equation $2,000 $A5/5 = FV$ = ($2,000) (5.526) = $11,052.
2. The $11,052 accumulation through the end of Year 5 must be compounded at 5 percent through Year 15 to determine the total amount of the $68,688 requirement met by the first five deposits. Use of the future value of 1 equation results in $11,052 $a10/5 = FV$ = ($11,052) (1.629) = $18,004.
3. The required annual deposit for the last ten years is calculated by solving the equation $X $A10/5 = FV$ = $50,684 ($68,688 − $18,004) = ($X) (12.578) = $50,684; $X = $4,030.

The parents must deposit $4,030 into the education account at the end of each of the last ten years during which the fund is accumulated.

Use of State College Savings Bonds

Regular state bonds are sold at par value and pay interest annually until maturity. Some states also issue college savings bonds which, like zero coupon bonds, are sold at a discount. In Washington state, for example, $50 million of education bonds were issued in 1988 with maturity dates ranging from seven to twenty years. Interest on the bonds is not subject to federal income tax. Therefore the rate set by the state on the bonds was the effective yield rate to be used in determining the purchase price of the bonds and their annual increase in value. For example, if the state offered a $10,000, fifteen-year bond at a rate of 6 percent, the purchase price could be determined by solving the equation for calculating the present value of 1 as follows: $10,000 $p15/6 = PV$ = ($10,000) (.417) = $4,170. Conversely, the future value of $4,170 when compounded at 6 percent for fifteen years is $10,000, that is, $4,170 $a15/6 = FV$ = ($4,170) (2.397) = $10,000 (rounded). The single deposit of $4,170 will provide $10,000 for education purposes at the end of Year 15.

Assume the $4,170 had instead been invested in a savings account earning 6 percent interest subject to federal income tax, thereby resulting in an after-tax yield of, for example, 4 percent. The total accumulation in the education fund after fifteen years would be only $7,510, calculated as follows: $4,170 $a15/4 = FV$ = ($4,170) (1.801) = $7,510. The net advantage of the state bonds becomes readily apparent. To have $10,000 avail-able for a child's education at the end of Year 15, parents would have to invest $5,552 in a fund with an after-tax earnings rate of 4 percent, calculated as follows: $X \, a15/4 = \$10,000 = FV = (\$X) \, (1.801) = \$10,000$; $\$X = \$5,552$. Note that this deposit is $1,382 ($5,552 − $4,170) greater than required to accumulate $10,000 at a 6 percent tax-free rate.

The amount of the immediate single deposit required to be made to a fund can also be determined using a present value of 1 calculation because it is the reverse, or reciprocal, of the future value of 1 calculation. For example, assume a family with a 40 percent income tax rate wants to know what dollar amount must be invested in ten-year, 6 percent state bonds with a maturity value of $40,000. The equation to solve the problem is $\$40,000 \, p10/6 = PV = (\$40,000) \, (.558) = \$22,320$, the amount the family must currently pay for the state bonds. The cash flow pattern is depicted by the following time line:

```
/-----/-----/-----/---  ... --/-----/
0     1     2     3    ...   9    10

                                 $40,000

PV   <-------------------------------
```

The family's education fund would have to earn a 10 percent return before taxes on taxable interest-bearing investments to earn an after-tax yield equal to the 6 percent tax-free interest on the state bonds. If only investments with 6 percent taxable earnings are available to the family, an amount much higher than the previously calculated $22,320 state bond investment would be required to provide a $40,000 education fund at the end of Year 10. The required investment can be calculated by solving the following present value of 1 equation: $\$40,000 \, p10/3.6 = PV$, where 3.6 is the after-tax return on the ten-year investment (6% − 40% lost to taxes). By interpolation, the $p10/3.6$ factor is determined to be .703. Substituting this factor into the equation, the calculation becomes ($40,000) (.703) = PV = $28,120, an immediate investment deposit $5,800 higher ($28,120 − $22,320) than required for the tax-free state bonds.

RETIREMENT ACCOUNTS

An individual's retirement income needs can be met in a number of ways, including use of social security payments, employer-sponsored pension plan benefits, and benefits available from personal investments in individual retirement accounts (IRAs) or other tax-sheltered investments, stock and mutual funds, savings accounts, cash surrender value of life insurance policies, and real estate, among others.

Determining Retirement Income Needs

The annual amount of retirement income benefits individuals need depends on their personal spending patterns and plans after retirement. Two approaches to determining retirement income requirements will be illustrated, one based on an explicit calculation of needs and the other on use of a ratio between retirement income and current income. In both cases, an adjustment will be made for inflation.

Assume an individual plans to start a retirement program that will provide ample income for him and his wife to continue their current lifestyle after their retirement at age 65. The couple, both age 45, has a combined income of $70,000, and their two children attend college. For simplicity, assume the couple has no prior savings or other potential retirement funds.

The following schedule provides a comparison of the couple's current annual spending versus what they project to be their needs each year during retirement measured in today's dollars:

Type of Expenditure	Current Spending	Projected Spending
Home mortgage, paid off at age 65	$ 7,200	$ 0
Property taxes and home insurance	1,400	1,400
Life insurance and noninsured medical care	1,000	1,000
Charitable contributions	3,000	1,000
Automobile payments (one auto after retirement)	8,000	4,200
Automobile insurance and expenses	4,000	2,000
Clothing	3,000	1,500
Grocery and household items	7,200	4,800
Vacations	3,000	3,000
College expenses	9,000	0
Social security taxes	5,000	0
Federal and state income tax	10,000	3,000
Contributions to employment pension plan	3,500	0
Miscellaneous expenses	2,000	2,000
Discretionary spending	2,700	3,100
Totals	$70,000	$27,000

In lieu of the $27,000 annual retirement need calculation, the couple might plan for a retirement income of about 50 percent of current earnings, or $35,000. In either case the calculated amount is expressed in current year dollars and must be adjusted for changes in purchasing power between now and age 65.

Adjustment for Changes in Purchasing Power

The consumer price index (CPI) for all urban consumers published by the U.S. Department of Labor is probably the most representative index available for adjusting projected retirement income needs of individuals. Between 1965 and 1985, the CPI rose from 94.5 to 322.2. To determine the compound rate of growth implicit in the CPI change, the equation for the future value of 1 can be used, as follows: 94.5 $a20/i$ = FV = 322.2, where $a20/i$ is the future value of 1 factor for twenty-one years at interest rate i. Solving the equation, $a20/i$ is calculated to be 3.410 (322.2 ÷ 94.5). Referring to the period 20 line of the "Future Value of $1" table, the factor 3.410 is found between the 6 and 7 percent columns. By interpolation, the rate is determined to be approximately 6.31 percent. If the rate of change in the purchasing power of the dollar is expected to be slightly less during the next twenty years than in the past twenty years, use of a 6 percent rate would seem appropriate. In fact, given that costs of housing and other major expenditures significantly affect the index, then a rate perhaps 30 to 50 percent lower might be justified.

Calculation of Retirement Fund Contributions

Assume that the 45-year-old couple with an annual retirement income need of $27,000 decides to adjust that amount to reflect a 5 percent annual change in the purchasing power of the dollar during the next twenty years. Their required annual retirement income therefore becomes $27,000 $a20/5$ = FV = ($27,000) (2.653) = $71,631. The following additional assumptions are made: changes in the purchasing power of the dollar subsequent to the couple's retirement age can be ignored; mortality tables show they will both live to age 80; the couple currently has no investments and savings; social security benefits will total $11,631 per year; investment funds will accumulate at an 8 percent rate.

After giving consideration to social security benefits, the couple must accumulate sufficient funds to provide for annual retirement income of $60,000. Assuming both principal and interest portions of the fund will be used to provide the $60,000, annual contributions to the retirement fund can be calculated.

First, the amount to be accumulated by age 65 should equal the present value of the $60,000 retirement annuity required by the couple for the fifteen-year period from age 65 to age 80. Using the general equation for calculating the present value of an ordinary annuity, the amount to be accumulated equals $60,000 $P15/8 = PV = (\$60,000) (8.559) = \$513,540$.

The amount of annual retirement fund contributions required to accumulate $513,540 can now be calculated using the general equation for the future value of an ordinary annuity. In this case the couple has twenty years (age 45 to age 65) to accumulate the required amount. Using the assumption of 8 percent earnings, the equation to be solved is X $A20/8 = FV = \$513,540$, where X is the required annual contribution. Substituting the $A20/8$ factor, the equation becomes $(\$X) (45.762) = \$513,540$, and $X = \$11,222$.

Having determined that $11,222 is to be invested each year for retirement, the couple must decide how to invest that amount to generate the after-tax earnings of 8 percent used in the calculations. In the illustration showing the calculation of the couple's $27,000 retirement income need, it was assumed they contributed $3,500 each year to an employer-sponsored pension plan. Assume the annual contributions are matched by the couple's employers and the pension fund generates tax-deferred earnings of 8 percent. In this case, $7,000 ($3,500 contribution + $3,500 employer match) of the $11,222 annual deposits required to accumulate $513,540 for retirement is satisfied. If annual contributions continue at that level and pension benefits become fully vested, the couple needs to invest only $4,222 more each year.

The couple has a variety of options for accumulating retirement income, which, among others, range from savings accounts, employer-sponsored pension plans, IRAs to corporate stock, real estate, and other investments, plus several combinations of the preceding. Each class of investment has a different level of risk as measured by the rate of return normally provided. For example, essentially risk-free passbook savings accounts yield about 5 percent interest; many stock investments may yield as much as 16 percent or more over certain time periods. Further, the tax status of various investments and funds differs. Municipal bond interest is exempt from federal income tax. Tax on pension fund and IRA earnings is normally deferred until amounts are withdrawn at retirement. Income taxes are paid currently on corporate dividends, while tax on the appreciation in a stock's value is deferred until the stock is sold.

Individuals or their personal financial planners must take these factors into consideration when selecting investment alternatives.

Other Factors Influencing Retirement Funds

Preceding calculations were based on the assumption that retirement income would be paid out of both principal and interest. Implicit in the calculations is that the couple would have no retirement income other than social security after age 80; the retirement fund would be reduced to zero. Several options are available to the couple to deal with this contingency. First, they can withdraw less than $60,000 each year and adapt to a lower standard of living. For example, if they withdraw only $52,306 each year, the $513,540 fund will last twenty years (to age 85) instead of fifteen years, calculated as follows: $X\ P20/8 = $513,540 = ($X)$ (9.818), and $X = $52,306 = retirement annuity for twenty years with 8 percent fund earnings.

A second alternative is to deposit more than the $11,222 amount required to provide a $60,000 annual retirement annuity. Another alternative is to use part or all of the retirement fund to purchase annuity contracts. Life insurance companies, for example, offer a variety of annuity options such as a fixed amount per year for life or an equal annual amount for ten years plus a reduced annual amount for life thereafter. In some cases the annuity payments continue for a certain period to a designated beneficiary after the death of one or both spouses, whereas in other cases nothing is paid after death. The annuity contract option selected influences the dollar amount of the payments.

These alternatives, and others, should be evaluated by those planning retirement programs. Consideration should be given to several factors influencing retirement accounts such as tax law changes, actual versus planned contributions and earnings rates, effects of transferring retirement contributions between funds and from one tax jurisdiction to another, and changes in general economic conditions, including rates of inflation. Certain retirement fund investment options that appear unattractive may prove desirable upon careful analysis. For example, use of present value analysis may reveal that penalty taxes on a premature IRA withdrawal may be outweighed by the dollar benefit of accumulating retirement funds under the tax-sheltered status. That is, the difference between the compound dollar growth of the fund without annual taxes versus with annual taxes may exceed the premature withdrawal penalty.

10

Other Uses of Present Value Analysis

This chapter completes the presentation on present value applications and is designed to satisfy two objectives: it applies present value analysis to legal settlements and considers unique applications of present value analysis.

LEGAL SETTLEMENTS

Numerous lawsuits filed in the United States include claims of wrongful death or injury. In cases involving the sole or primary provider of family income, the outcome of such suits can have a significant effect on the living conditions and life-style of family members. In fact, the latter often seek compensation for loss of companionship and income.

The dollar amounts of claims in injury cases normally depend on the earning power lost and the length of time an injury is expected to persist. In some situations, losses are mitigated by the ability of those injured to find alternative employment. Wrongful death claims require measuring lost earnings for the period of time a deceased would have worked until retirement. Further, retirement income potential must be determined making reference to mortality tables.

Regardless of the nature of claims, whether by a family, business, or other litigant, present value analysis is required. In all cases cash flow estimates must be made of potential future earnings of the injured or deceased less ordinary and reasonable costs and expenses. Net cash flows must then be discounted to their present value using an appropriate discount rate for the number of time periods involved. A simplified example will be used to demonstrate the basic analysis required in computing the amount of a wrongful death or injury claim.

Assume that a married man with no children is killed at the age of 55 and that he was a sole wage earner. His annual income from employment at the time of death was $45,000. Further, assume normal retirement age in his occupation is 65 and that mortality tables indicate that his life expectancy was 80 years of age. He was killed accidentally because of purported negligence of the company or individual to be sued.

The dollar amount of the claim should be based on a calculation of the present value of future wages and other benefits that would have accrued to the deceased and his wife had he not been killed. In this example, only the present value of future wages is considered; however, benefits such as earnings from supplemental sources and cost savings to the household for repair and maintenance services performed by the deceased should also be included. Calculations should reflect lost retirement income and insurance benefits and the wife's emotional trauma. Appropriate deductions should be made for social security and life insurance death benefits plus cost savings for food, clothing, and so forth subsequent to death plus the effects of state and federal income and other taxes. In short, the cash flows to be discounted are analogous to incremental after-tax cash flow calculations (ATCF) discussed in earlier chapters.

The quality of a claim filed will be a function of how carefully the income and expense variables associated with a given death and subsequent time periods are considered and measured. The deceased's potential income must be forecasted. Salary estimates have to be based on reasonable and normally expected promotions plus adjustments for inflation. Other pertinent adjustments to reflect the specific job may have to be made. The process requires an intimate knowledge of the deceased's job, work, and life habits.

This approach to forecasting is similar to that performed regularly by business organizations in, for example, projecting future potential of long-term markets for a product or service. Estimates of cash flows and required long-term investments have to be made based on reasonable and normal assumptions. Probable future cash flows must take precedence over pure speculation in computing a range of reasonable amounts on which to base claims.

In this case, it will be assumed that the increments added annually to the deceased's salary did not always keep up with inflation and that no promotions could reasonably have been expected over the next ten years. Historical salary records reveal annual salary increases of 3 percent, the rate that future projections will be based on. Given these assumptions, the next year's salary would have been $56,350 ($45,000 x 1.03). Of that amount it is estimated that the deceased's personal expenses for food, clothing, medical, fuel, and other miscellaneous expenses would be 20 percent of salary, or $9,270. Total taxes (income, real estate, and others) are estimated at 35 percent of salary. Similar analysis must be made for benefits in the years to retirement. Table 10.1 summarizes these calculations.

Two further adjustments have to be made to these numbers. The first one is to determine the probability the deceased would have lived from age 55 to age 65. Assuming mortality (life expectancy) tables show a 90 percent probability, then only that percentage of the "Net Dollars to Spouse" column in Table 10.1 should be discounted. The second adjustment involves funds that would be received after age 65, for example, social security payments. If mortality tables showed that this individual's life expectancy was 80 years, social security payments would have been received from age 65 to 80. These amounts would have to be adjusted by the probability of death from age 65 to 80 and reduced by social security payments available to the spouse. Personal expenses of the deceased and income taxes would also have to be deducted. For these reasons, an appropriate cash flow schedule would show future dollars to be discounted from one year (age 56) to twenty-five years (age 80). To simplify this illustration, only the time period from age 55 to 65 is considered. Table 10.2 shows the adjustment to 90 percent and the present value calculations for the ten-year period.

Since the time span is ten years, the current ten-year treasury bond rate of 9 percent was used as the discount rate. The present value of $135,216 reflects the dollar amount of the wrongful death claim in this

TABLE 10.1
Projected Net Loss of Earning Power, Wrongful Death Claim

Age	Expected Salary	Taxes and Expenses	Dollars to Spouse
56	$46,350	$25,492	$20,858
57	47,740	26,257	21,483
58	49,172	27,045	22,127
59	50,647	27,856	22,791
60	52,166	28,691	23,475
61	53,731	29,552	24,179
62	55,343	30,439	24,904
63	57,003	31,352	25,651
64	58,713	32,292	26,421
65	60,474	33,261	27,213

TABLE 10.2
Present Value of Lost Earning Power, Wrongful Death Claim

Age	Net Dollars to Spouse*	90% Probability Adjustment	9% Discount Factor	Present Value
56	$20,858	$18,722	0.917	$17,214
57	21,483	19,335	0.842	16,280
58	22,127	19,914	0.772	15,374
59	22,791	20,512	0.708	14,522
60	23,475	21,128	0.650	13,733
61	24,179	21,761	0.596	12,970
62	24,904	22,414	0.547	12,260
63	25,651	23,036	0.502	11,589
64	26,421	23,799	0.460	10,938
65	27,213	24,492	0.422	10,336
	Present value of lost earnings			$135,216

* from Table 10.1

case. If the future social security payments had been included for ages 65 to 80, then the table would have shown twenty-five years (age 55–80) of cash flows to discount and the appropriate rate would have been a twenty-five-year treasury bond rate. Of course, the claim would be for a higher dollar amount.

One of us worked on a wrongful death case several years ago. After I explained that I had selected an appropriate treasury bond rate to discount future earnings, the opposition attorney on cross-examination asked why a treasury bill rate had not been selected. I responded, "Because we would have sued you for more money." The attorney, realizing his mistake, claimed the response was irrelevant and immaterial and wanted it stricken from the record. The jury, however, had already surmised that the attorney had not prepared sufficiently for the case. The point of the incident is that the higher the discount rate applied to future cash flows is, the lower their present value will be. Since the treasury bill rate is normally lower than treasury bond rates, the dollar claim will be higher if the present value of cash flows is discounted using the treasury bill rate.

Note that the example used earlier was based on consideration of only future potential income loss to age 65 and resulted in a dollar claim for the estate or wife of $135,216. Had the step of calculating the present value of future social security payments been included, possibly the damages claimed in the lawsuit would have exceeded $200,000. Nonetheless, the example illustrates the importance of projecting future potential income loss due to the death. Additional damages for loss of love and affection should also be included. Consideration of all relevant factors in wrongful death and injury suits can lead to the award of high dollar damages.

The points we have discussed may be equally applicable to defendants. For example, a business or individual named as a defendant in a wrongful death lawsuit must be familiar with the plaintiff's method of calculating losses so that alternative calculations can be made to minimize potential losses. A business might decide that the cost of its loss in a given case can be reduced by offering an annuity to the plaintiff. The present value of the annuity might be less than an amount awarded by a judge or jury, and legal costs can be kept to a minimum.

If a business is a plaintiff in a given case, of course, it would apply principles similar to those used by an individual. However, losses would be measured in terms of business interruption costs or other net cash outflows or reduced cash inflows caused by the action giving rise to the loss. For example, the present value of the loss arising from equipment damaged can be measured using the cash flows estimated in the equipment acquisition decision.

OTHER APPLICATIONS OF PRESENT VALUE ANALYSIS

Awarding of Prizes

Businesses often use prizes to stimulate sales of a product. Cereal companies and others have long offered premiums to individuals or groups who turn in product box tops or labels. In these cases, there is very little time lag between the date of sale and the redemption date. Thus, the cost of the promotion can be readily determined without discounting related cash flows to their present value. Some companies, however, offer major cash prizes paid over several time periods. Consider the following example.

A fast food chain sponsored a game in which customers could win Prize A of $15,000 a year for ten years, Prize B of $100,000 a year for life, among other prizes. Present value analysis can be used to determine the cost of the promotion. To illustrate, assume that the company awarded ten of Prize A and two of Prize B (and no other prizes). Assume that the lifetime prizes were won by individuals who were both 35 years old (an assumed average-age customer) and expected to live to age 75. The company can fund the prizes by purchasing annuity contracts that provide for a 10 percent annual rate of return. Therefore, payments to the individuals should be discounted at 10 percent. The present value will equal the cost of the annuities and, hence, the cost of the promotion.

The cost can be calculated by discounting the future cash flows using the general equation for the present value of an annuity, as follows:

Prize A (ten prizes of $15,000 a year for ten years): $150,000 $P10/10$ = PV = $150,000) (6.145) = $921,750 = present value cost of the A prizes.

Prize B (two prizes of $100,000 a year for forty years — age 35 to age 75): $200,000 $P40/10$ = PV = ($200,000) (9.779) = $1,955,800 = present value cost of the B prize.

Based on the preceding calculations, the total cost to the company of the promotion is $2,877,550 ($921,750 + $1,955,800). Factors the company had to consider before deciding to sponsor the promotion included advertising, cost of the game pieces, probability that all prizes would be distributed, increase in revenues and profits arising from the promotion, and others. Note that the promotion decision is essentially a capital budgeting problem. If increased cash flow from sales exceeds the present value cost of the promotion, the promotion should be sponsored.

State Lotteries

State lotteries can be evaluated in the same manner as the sales promotion. Assume a state is interested in sponsoring a lottery and estimates that sales of lottery tickets each year will total $30 million. Annual costs of administering the program are expected to total $5 million. Rules proposed for the lottery require the state to pay the winners over a twenty-year period an absolute dollar amount equal to the $30 million in ticket sales. The state can purchase an annuity contract providing 10 percent interest to satisfy its obligation to the winner.

The state's decision to sponsor or not sponsor the lottery should be based on a present value analysis in which the $5 million administration cost plus the present value of the annuities awarded the winners is compared to the $30 million in ticket sales. The $1.5 million annuity ($30 million ÷ 20 years) should be discounted at 10 percent, as follows: $1.5 million $P20/10$ = PV = cost of annuity = ($1.5 million) (8.514) = $12.771 million. Therefore, the lottery should be sponsored, a decision supported by the following computations (in millions of dollars):

Receipts from sale of lottery tickets		$30.000
Disbursements for lottery		
Administration	$ 5.000	
Annuity contract	12.771	17.771
Excess of receipts over disbursements		$12.229

Low Interest Financing

Options for buyers to elect cash rebates or low interest financing when purchasing a new automobile have been discussed. Now we focus on the use of low interest financing alone as a means for a seller to stimulate sales. From the seller's viewpoint, the decision may be to conduct sales in which merchandise is offered at 10 to 25 percent off the usual price or in which customers may be given interest-free or low interest financing. Consider the following example.

A furniture retailer operates in a highly competitive market. It charges 12 percent annual interest to customers who finance their purchases under the company's twelve-month and twenty-four-month installment note plans. The retailer wants to promote sales of a $3,000 living room set by offering either two-year, 6 percent financing or a 10 percent cash discount.

The low interest option reduces the buyer's monthly payments by $8, determined by comparing solutions to the following two equations. First, $X P24/0.5 = $3,000 = PV = ($X) (22.563) = $3,000, and $X = $133 = the monthly payment using 6 percent financing. Second, $X P24/1 = $3,000 = PV = ($X) (21.243) = $3,000, and $X = $141 = monthly payment using 12 percent financing. Discounting the $8 reduction in monthly payments for two years at the seller's 12 percent opportunity rate, the present value cost of low interest financing is $170 ($8 P24/1 = PV = $8 x 21.243). Since this amount is less than the $300 cost of offering a 10 percent discount ($3,000 selling price x 10%), the seller should offer customers low interest financing.

If customers perceive that the low interest rate is equivalent to about a 5 percent cash discount, the seller may have to offer no interest (free) financing. The cost of free financing is computed by first comparing the $141 monthly payment under 12 percent financing with the $125 monthly payment ($3,000 ÷ 24 months) if no interest is charged. The $16 difference in monthly payments is then discounted at 12 percent: $16 P24/1 = PV = ($16) (21.243) = $340 = present value cost of interest-free financing, an amount equal to about an 11 percent sales discount. Therefore customers should be offered a 10 percent discount rather than the no interest option. However, the cost difference is so minimal that sales might be increased further by offering customers both options.

Effect of Compound Growth Rates on Wages and Salaries

The interrelationship that exists among wage rates, absolute dollar wage increases, and compound wage growth is dynamic. Interaction among the three factors can result in dramatic wage differentials. Increases in the base dollar amount of wages and salaries paid to employees have profound implication for future pay increases. Consider a firm that in 1970 paid an average salary of $10,000 to new staff and granted a 10 percent pay increase after the first year of service. If the firm had fifty new staff members, the cost of the pay increase would be $50,000 (50 staff x a $1,000 pay increase for each). Assume that by 1988 (eighteen years later) salaries for first-year staff had increased to $24,000. Three points should be observed:

1. Entry-level salaries have increased at a compound annual growth rate of about 5 percent ($10,000 $a18/i = FV$ = $24,000: $a18/i$ = 2.400 = 5% factor for eighteen periods in the "Future Value of 1" table).
2. The cost of funding a 10 percent pay increase at the end of one year of service in 1988 for fifty employees has risen to $120,000 (50 employees x $2,400 pay increase) from $50,000.
3. Staff hired in 1970 would have to receive annual pay increases averaging greater than 5 percent per year just to keep ahead of new staff.

Allowing for eighteen years' experience among other factors, assume 1970 staff are in 1988 earning $40,000 per year, representing a compound growth rate in salaries of 8 percent ($10,000 $a18/i = FV$ = $40,000, and $a18/i$ = 4.000, the future value of 1 factor for about 8 percent on the period 18 line). Note that while entry-level salaries have increased at a constant rate (5 percent) each year, the absolute dollar increase each year is not constant. That is, a 10 percent increase in the salary of a new staff member in 1970 cost $1,000 ($10,000 salary x 10%) compared to $2,400 ($24,000 salary x 10%) in 1988. Further, an 8 percent increase in the 1988 salary of a staff member hired in 1970 will cost $3,200 ($40,000 salary x 8%). Thus in a relatively short time, the total dollar salary cost for a firm may increase dramatically. Taking a broader view, it can be seen that continued use of equal percentage increases in salaries has implications both between companies and within companies for different wage classes of employees, as well as among individuals in the economy.

These observations should not be alarming to employers if revenues rise correspondingly and competitors face a similar situation. However, competitors may offer a substitute product or service or may operate in a country where corresponding salaries are at much lower equivalent dollar amounts. Particularly in the latter case, competitors will have much lower overall salary costs in the short run and long run, even if other salary costs increase at the same annual rate. Similar circumstances have prompted companies to become more productive or more highly automated, to modify wage agreements, or to relocate operations to foreign countries or other parts of the United States where salary and wage levels are lower.

Key Employee Salary Negotiations

Large organizations, sports franchises, and other operations frequently must deal with unique individuals who command premium salaries. One approach to negotiating with them is to take advantage of the effects of the time value of money. That is, to the extent payment of a starting salary or bonus can be deferred to a later period, a company may be able to offer a higher gross salary as a means of attracting or retaining a key employee.

An article written by John Clayton and appearing in the August 16, 1987, edition of *The Spokesman-Review* illustrates the point. Clayton writes of the contract offer received by Brian Bosworth from the Seattle Seahawks professional football team and compares it to offers received by other professional athletes. The following time line illustrates the cash payments, in thousands of dollars, due each year to Bosworth under the contract:

```
        /-----/-----/-----/-----/-----/-----/-----/
        0     1     2     3     4     5     6     7
Salary: $300  $400  $500  $600  $700 $1000 $1100


        /-----/-----/-----/-----/-----/-----/
        8     9    10    11    12    13    14
       $1200 $1300 $1400
Signing Bonus:              $500  $500  $500  $500

    PV  <--------------------------------------------
```

The absolute dollars payable under the contract total $10,500 ($300 + $400 + ... + $1,400 + $500 + $500 + $500 + $500), or $10.5 million. Using the equation for the present value of a deferred annuity, it can be seen that the signing bonus was worth $767,000 and that the total salary was worth $5,152,800 in terms of dollars required in 1987 to sign Bosworth to the contract, assuming an 8 percent discount rate. The calculations are as follows: Salary $= PV = \$300\,p1/8 + \$400\,p2/8 + ... + \$1,400\,p10/8 = (\$300)\,(.926) + (\$400)\,(.857) + ... + (\$1,400)\,(.463) = \$5,152,800$, and bonus $= PV = (\$500)\,(P14/8 - P10/8) = (\$500)\,(8.244 - 6.701) = (\$500)\,(1.534) = \$767,000$. Use of a higher interest rate to discount cash flows will result in lower present values. (Bosworth's agent used a 10 percent discount rate.)

Although many professional athletes command uniquely high salaries, the principles illustrated in the case have many applications. Deferred payment contracts can be offered not only to key employees but to other companies in purchase negotiations, among other circumstances.

Appendix

Factors for use in making calculations of present and future values of cash flows are contained in this appendix. Readers are cautioned that all factors are rounded to three decimal places. Computations involving large dollar amounts, several compounding periods, and high interest rates should be made using a computer or programmable calculator in cases requiring a high degree of accuracy. The four tables presented are summarized as follows:

Future Value of $1 — used to determine the future value of a single given sum at the end of n periods compounded at a specified interest rate;

Present Value of $1 — used to determine the value now of a single given sum due n periods hence discounted at a specified compound interest rate;

Future Value of an Ordinary Annuity of $1 — used to determine the accumulated future value of a series of equal payments made each period for n periods and compounded at a specified interest rate;

Present Value of an Ordinary Annuity of $1 — used to determine the value now of a series of equal payments made each period for n periods and discounted at a specified compound interest rate.

Future Value of $1

Periods	0.5%	1%	1.5%	2%	3%	4%	5%	6%	7%	8%	9%	10%	12%	14%	16%	18%	20%
1	1.005	1.010	1.015	1.020	1.030	1.040	1.050	1.060	1.070	1.080	1.090	1.100	1.120	1.140	1.160	1.180	1.200
2	1.010	1.020	1.030	1.040	1.061	1.082	1.103	1.124	1.145	1.166	1.188	1.210	1.254	1.300	1.346	1.392	1.440
3	1.015	1.030	1.046	1.061	1.093	1.125	1.158	1.191	1.225	1.260	1.295	1.331	1.405	1.482	1.561	1.643	1.728
4	1.020	1.041	1.061	1.082	1.126	1.170	1.216	1.262	1.311	1.360	1.412	1.464	1.574	1.689	1.811	1.939	2.074
5	1.025	1.051	1.077	1.104	1.159	1.217	1.276	1.338	1.403	1.469	1.539	1.611	1.762	1.925	2.100	2.288	2.488
6	1.030	1.062	1.093	1.126	1.194	1.265	1.340	1.419	1.501	1.587	1.677	1.772	1.974	2.195	2.436	2.700	2.986
7	1.036	1.072	1.110	1.149	1.230	1.316	1.407	1.504	1.606	1.714	1.828	1.949	2.211	2.502	2.826	3.185	3.583
8	1.041	1.083	1.126	1.172	1.267	1.369	1.477	1.594	1.718	1.851	1.993	2.144	2.476	2.853	3.278	3.759	4.300
9	1.046	1.094	1.143	1.195	1.305	1.423	1.551	1.689	1.838	1.999	2.172	2.358	2.773	3.252	3.803	4.435	5.160
10	1.051	1.105	1.161	1.219	1.344	1.480	1.629	1.791	1.967	2.159	2.367	2.594	3.106	3.707	4.411	5.234	6.192
11	1.056	1.116	1.178	1.243	1.384	1.539	1.710	1.898	2.105	2.332	2.580	2.853	3.479	4.226	5.117	6.176	7.430
12	1.062	1.127	1.196	1.268	1.426	1.601	1.796	2.012	2.252	2.518	2.813	3.138	3.896	4.818	5.936	7.288	8.916
13	1.067	1.138	1.214	1.294	1.469	1.665	1.886	2.133	2.410	2.720	3.066	3.452	4.363	5.492	6.886	8.599	10.699
14	1.072	1.149	1.232	1.319	1.513	1.732	1.980	2.261	2.579	2.937	3.342	3.797	4.887	6.261	7.988	10.147	12.839
15	1.078	1.161	1.250	1.346	1.558	1.801	2.079	2.397	2.759	3.172	3.642	4.177	5.474	7.138	9.266	11.974	15.407
16	1.083	1.173	1.269	1.373	1.605	1.873	2.183	2.540	2.952	3.426	3.970	4.595	6.130	8.137	10.748	14.129	18.488
18	1.094	1.196	1.307	1.428	1.702	2.026	2.407	2.854	3.380	3.996	4.717	5.560	7.690	10.575	14.463	19.673	26.623
20	1.105	1.220	1.347	1.486	1.806	2.191	2.653	3.207	3.870	4.661	5.604	6.727	9.646	13.743	19.461	27.393	38.338
22	1.116	1.245	1.388	1.546	1.916	2.370	2.925	3.604	4.430	5.437	6.659	8.140	12.100	17.861	26.186	38.142	55.206
24	1.127	1.270	1.430	1.608	2.033	2.563	3.225	4.049	5.072	6.341	7.911	9.850	15.179	23.212	35.236	53.109	79.497
26	1.138	1.295	1.473	1.673	2.157	2.772	3.556	4.549	5.807	7.396	9.399	11.918	19.040	30.167	47.414	73.949	114.475
28	1.150	1.321	1.517	1.741	2.288	2.999	3.920	5.112	6.649	8.627	11.167	14.421	23.884	39.204	63.800	102.967	164.845
30	1.161	1.348	1.563	1.811	2.427	3.243	4.322	5.743	7.612	10.063	13.268	17.449	29.960	50.950	85.850	143.371	237.376
32	1.173	1.375	1.610	1.885	2.575	3.508	4.765	6.453	8.715	11.737	15.763	21.114	37.582	66.215	115.520	199.629	341.822
34	1.185	1.403	1.659	1.961	2.732	3.794	5.253	7.251	9.978	13.690	18.728	25.548	47.143	86.053	155.443	277.964	492.224
36	1.197	1.431	1.709	2.040	2.898	4.104	5.792	8.147	11.424	15.968	22.251	30.913	59.136	111.834	209.164	387.037	708.802
40	1.221	1.489	1.814	2.208	3.262	4.801	7.040	10.286	14.974	21.725	31.409	45.259	93.051	188.884	378.721	750.378	1469.722
44	1.245	1.549	1.925	2.390	3.671	5.617	8.557	12.985	19.628	29.556	44.337	66.264	146.418	319.017	685.727	1454.817	3047.718
48	1.270	1.612	2.043	2.587	4.132	6.571	10.401	16.394	25.729	40.211	62.585	97.017	230.391	538.807	1241.605	2820.567	6319.749

Present Value of $1

Periods	0.5%	1%	1.5%	2%	3%	4%	5%	6%	7%	8%	9%	10%	12%	14%	16%	18%	20%
1	0.995	0.990	0.985	0.980	0.971	0.962	0.952	0.943	0.935	0.926	0.917	0.909	0.893	0.877	0.862	0.847	0.833
2	0.990	0.980	0.971	0.961	0.943	0.925	0.907	0.890	0.873	0.857	0.842	0.826	0.797	0.769	0.743	0.718	0.694
3	0.985	0.971	0.956	0.942	0.915	0.889	0.864	0.840	0.816	0.794	0.772	0.751	0.712	0.675	0.641	0.609	0.579
4	0.980	0.961	0.942	0.924	0.888	0.855	0.823	0.792	0.763	0.735	0.708	0.683	0.636	0.592	0.552	0.516	0.482
5	0.975	0.951	0.928	0.906	0.863	0.822	0.784	0.747	0.713	0.681	0.650	0.621	0.567	0.519	0.476	0.437	0.402
6	0.971	0.942	0.915	0.888	0.837	0.790	0.746	0.705	0.666	0.630	0.596	0.564	0.507	0.456	0.410	0.370	0.335
7	0.966	0.933	0.901	0.871	0.813	0.760	0.711	0.665	0.623	0.583	0.547	0.513	0.452	0.400	0.354	0.314	0.279
8	0.961	0.923	0.888	0.853	0.789	0.731	0.677	0.627	0.582	0.540	0.502	0.467	0.404	0.351	0.305	0.266	0.233
9	0.956	0.914	0.875	0.837	0.766	0.703	0.645	0.592	0.544	0.500	0.460	0.424	0.361	0.308	0.263	0.225	0.194
10	0.951	0.905	0.862	0.820	0.744	0.676	0.614	0.558	0.508	0.463	0.422	0.386	0.322	0.270	0.227	0.191	0.162
11	0.947	0.896	0.849	0.804	0.722	0.650	0.585	0.527	0.475	0.429	0.388	0.350	0.287	0.237	0.195	0.162	0.135
12	0.942	0.887	0.836	0.788	0.701	0.625	0.557	0.497	0.444	0.397	0.356	0.319	0.257	0.208	0.168	0.137	0.112
13	0.937	0.879	0.824	0.773	0.681	0.601	0.530	0.469	0.415	0.368	0.326	0.290	0.229	0.182	0.145	0.116	0.093
14	0.933	0.870	0.812	0.758	0.661	0.577	0.505	0.442	0.388	0.340	0.299	0.263	0.205	0.160	0.125	0.099	0.078
15	0.928	0.861	0.800	0.743	0.642	0.555	0.481	0.417	0.362	0.315	0.275	0.239	0.183	0.140	0.108	0.084	0.065
16	0.923	0.853	0.788	0.728	0.623	0.534	0.458	0.394	0.339	0.292	0.252	0.218	0.163	0.123	0.093	0.071	0.054
18	0.914	0.836	0.765	0.700	0.587	0.494	0.416	0.350	0.296	0.250	0.212	0.180	0.130	0.095	0.069	0.051	0.038
20	0.905	0.820	0.742	0.673	0.554	0.456	0.377	0.312	0.258	0.215	0.178	0.149	0.104	0.073	0.051	0.037	0.026
22	0.896	0.803	0.721	0.647	0.522	0.422	0.342	0.278	0.226	0.184	0.150	0.123	0.083	0.056	0.038	0.026	0.018
24	0.887	0.788	0.700	0.622	0.492	0.390	0.310	0.247	0.197	0.158	0.126	0.102	0.066	0.043	0.028	0.019	0.013
26	0.878	0.772	0.679	0.598	0.464	0.361	0.281	0.220	0.172	0.135	0.106	0.084	0.053	0.033	0.021	0.014	0.009
28	0.870	0.757	0.659	0.574	0.437	0.333	0.255	0.196	0.150	0.116	0.090	0.069	0.042	0.026	0.016	0.010	0.006
30	0.861	0.742	0.640	0.552	0.412	0.308	0.231	0.174	0.131	0.099	0.075	0.057	0.033	0.020	0.012	0.007	0.004
32	0.852	0.727	0.621	0.531	0.388	0.285	0.210	0.155	0.115	0.085	0.063	0.047	0.027	0.015	0.009	0.005	0.003
34	0.844	0.713	0.603	0.510	0.366	0.264	0.190	0.138	0.100	0.073	0.053	0.039	0.021	0.012	0.006	0.004	0.002
36	0.836	0.699	0.585	0.490	0.345	0.244	0.173	0.123	0.088	0.063	0.045	0.032	0.017	0.009	0.005	0.003	0.001
40	0.819	0.672	0.551	0.453	0.307	0.208	0.142	0.097	0.067	0.046	0.032	0.022	0.011	0.005	0.003	0.001	0.001
44	0.803	0.645	0.519	0.418	0.272	0.178	0.117	0.077	0.051	0.034	0.023	0.015	0.007	0.003	0.001	0.001	<.001
48	0.787	0.620	0.489	0.387	0.242	0.152	0.096	0.061	0.039	0.025	0.016	0.010	0.004	0.002	0.001	<.001	<.001

Future Value of an Ordinary Annuity of $1

Payments	0.5%	1%	1.5%	2%	3%	4%	5%	6%	7%	8%	9%	10%	12%	14%	16%	18%	20%
1	1.000	1.000	1.000	1.000	1.000	1.000	1.000	1.000	1.000	1.000	1.000	1.000	1.000	1.000	1.000	1.000	1.000
2	2.005	2.010	2.015	2.020	2.030	2.040	2.050	2.060	2.070	2.080	2.090	2.100	2.120	2.140	2.160	2.180	2.200
3	3.015	3.030	3.045	3.060	3.091	3.122	3.153	3.184	3.215	3.246	3.278	3.310	3.374	3.440	3.506	3.572	3.640
4	4.030	4.060	4.091	4.122	4.184	4.246	4.310	4.375	4.440	4.506	4.573	4.641	4.779	4.921	5.066	5.215	5.368
5	5.050	5.101	5.152	5.204	5.309	5.416	5.526	5.637	5.751	5.867	5.985	6.105	6.353	6.610	6.877	7.154	7.442
6	6.076	6.152	6.230	6.308	6.468	6.633	6.802	6.975	7.153	7.336	7.523	7.716	8.115	8.536	8.977	9.442	9.930
7	7.106	7.214	7.323	7.434	7.662	7.898	8.142	8.394	8.654	8.923	9.200	9.487	10.089	10.730	11.414	12.142	12.916
8	8.141	8.286	8.433	8.583	8.892	9.214	9.549	9.897	10.260	10.637	11.028	11.436	12.300	13.233	14.240	15.327	16.499
9	9.182	9.369	9.559	9.755	10.159	10.583	11.027	11.491	11.978	12.488	13.021	13.579	14.776	16.085	17.519	19.085	20.799
10	10.228	10.462	10.703	10.950	11.464	12.006	12.578	13.181	13.816	14.487	15.193	15.937	17.549	19.337	21.321	23.521	25.959
11	11.279	11.567	11.863	12.169	12.808	13.486	14.207	14.972	15.784	16.645	17.560	18.531	20.655	23.045	25.733	28.755	32.150
12	12.336	12.683	13.041	13.412	14.192	15.026	15.917	16.870	17.888	18.977	20.141	21.384	24.133	27.271	30.850	34.931	39.581
13	13.397	13.809	14.237	14.680	15.618	16.627	17.713	18.882	20.141	21.495	22.953	24.523	28.029	32.089	36.786	42.219	48.497
14	14.464	14.947	15.450	15.974	17.086	18.292	19.599	21.015	22.550	24.215	26.019	27.975	32.393	37.581	43.672	50.818	59.196
15	15.537	16.097	16.682	17.293	18.599	20.024	21.579	23.276	25.129	27.152	29.361	31.772	37.280	43.842	51.660	60.965	72.035
16	16.614	17.258	17.932	18.639	20.157	21.825	23.657	25.673	27.888	30.324	33.003	35.950	42.753	50.980	60.925	72.939	87.442
18	18.786	19.615	20.489	21.412	23.414	25.645	28.132	30.906	33.999	37.450	41.301	45.599	55.750	68.394	84.141	103.740	128.117
20	20.979	22.019	23.124	24.297	26.870	29.778	33.066	36.786	40.995	45.762	51.160	57.275	72.052	91.025	115.380	146.628	186.688
22	23.194	24.472	25.838	27.299	30.537	34.248	38.505	43.392	49.006	55.457	62.873	71.403	92.503	120.436	157.415	206.345	271.031
24	25.432	26.973	28.634	30.422	34.426	39.083	44.502	50.816	58.177	66.765	76.790	88.497	118.155	158.659	213.978	289.494	392.484
26	27.692	29.526	31.514	33.671	38.553	44.312	51.113	59.156	68.676	79.954	93.324	109.182	150.334	208.333	290.088	405.272	567.377
28	29.975	32.129	34.481	37.051	42.931	49.968	58.403	68.528	80.698	95.339	112.968	134.210	190.699	272.889	392.503	566.481	819.223
30	32.280	34.785	37.539	40.568	47.575	56.085	66.439	79.058	94.461	113.283	136.308	164.494	241.333	356.787	530.312	790.948	1181.832
32	34.609	37.494	40.688	44.227	52.503	62.701	75.299	90.890	110.218	134.214	164.037	201.138	304.848	465.820	715.747	1103.496	1704.109
34	36.961	40.258	43.933	48.034	57.730	69.858	85.067	104.184	128.259	158.627	196.982	245.477	384.521	607.520	965.270	1538.688	2456.118
36	39.336	43.077	47.276	51.994	63.276	77.598	95.836	119.121	148.913	187.102	236.125	299.127	484.463	791.673	1301.027	2144.649	3539.009
40	44.159	48.886	54.268	60.402	75.401	95.026	120.800	154.762	199.635	259.057	337.882	442.593	767.091	1342.025	2360.757	4163.213	7343.858
44	49.079	54.932	61.689	69.503	89.048	115.413	151.143	199.758	266.121	356.950	481.322	652.641	1211.813	2271.548	4279.546	8076.760	15233.592
48	54.098	61.223	69.565	79.354	104.408	139.263	188.025	256.565	353.270	490.132	684.280	960.172	1911.590	3841.475	7753.782	15664.259	31593.744

Present Value of an Ordinary Annuity of $1

Payments	0.5%	1%	1.5%	2%	3%	4%	5%	6%	7%	8%	9%	10%	12%	14%	16%	18%	20%
1	0.995	0.990	0.985	0.980	0.971	0.962	0.952	0.943	0.935	0.926	0.917	0.909	0.893	0.877	0.862	0.847	0.833
2	1.985	1.970	1.956	1.942	1.913	1.886	1.859	1.833	1.808	1.783	1.759	1.736	1.690	1.647	1.605	1.566	1.528
3	2.970	2.941	2.912	2.884	2.829	2.775	2.723	2.673	2.624	2.577	2.531	2.487	2.402	2.322	2.246	2.174	2.106
4	3.950	3.902	3.854	3.808	3.717	3.630	3.546	3.465	3.387	3.312	3.240	3.170	3.037	2.914	2.798	2.690	2.589
5	4.926	4.853	4.783	4.713	4.580	4.452	4.329	4.212	4.100	3.993	3.890	3.791	3.605	3.433	3.274	3.127	2.991
6	5.896	5.795	5.697	5.601	5.417	5.242	5.076	4.917	4.767	4.623	4.486	4.355	4.111	3.889	3.685	3.498	3.326
7	6.862	6.728	6.598	6.472	6.230	6.002	5.786	5.582	5.389	5.206	5.033	4.868	4.564	4.288	4.039	3.812	3.605
8	7.823	7.652	7.486	7.325	7.020	6.733	6.463	6.210	5.971	5.747	5.535	5.335	4.968	4.639	4.344	4.078	3.837
9	8.779	8.566	8.361	8.162	7.786	7.435	7.108	6.802	6.515	6.247	5.995	5.759	5.328	4.946	4.607	4.303	4.031
10	9.730	9.471	9.222	8.983	8.530	8.111	7.722	7.360	7.024	6.710	6.418	6.145	5.650	5.216	4.833	4.494	4.192
11	10.677	10.368	10.071	9.787	9.253	8.760	8.306	7.887	7.499	7.139	6.805	6.495	5.937	5.453	5.029	4.656	4.327
12	11.619	11.255	10.908	10.575	9.954	9.385	8.863	8.384	7.943	7.536	7.161	6.814	6.194	5.660	5.197	4.793	4.439
13	12.556	12.134	11.732	11.348	10.635	9.986	9.394	8.853	8.358	7.904	7.487	7.103	6.424	5.842	5.342	4.910	4.533
14	13.489	13.004	12.543	12.106	11.296	10.563	9.899	9.295	8.745	8.244	7.786	7.367	6.628	6.002	5.468	5.008	4.611
15	14.417	13.865	13.343	12.849	11.938	11.118	10.380	9.712	9.108	8.559	8.061	7.606	6.811	6.142	5.575	5.092	4.675
16	15.340	14.718	14.131	13.578	12.561	11.652	10.838	10.106	9.447	8.851	8.313	7.824	6.974	6.265	5.668	5.162	4.730
18	17.173	16.398	15.673	14.992	13.754	12.659	11.690	10.828	10.059	9.372	8.756	8.201	7.250	6.467	5.818	5.273	4.812
20	18.987	18.046	17.169	16.351	14.877	13.590	12.462	11.470	10.594	9.818	9.129	8.514	7.469	6.623	5.929	5.353	4.870
22	20.784	19.660	18.621	17.658	15.937	14.451	13.163	12.042	11.061	10.201	9.442	8.772	7.645	6.743	6.011	5.410	4.909
24	22.563	21.243	20.030	18.914	16.936	15.247	13.799	12.550	11.469	10.529	9.707	8.985	7.784	6.835	6.073	5.451	4.937
26	24.324	22.795	21.399	20.121	17.877	15.983	14.375	13.003	11.826	10.810	9.929	9.161	7.896	6.906	6.118	5.480	4.956
28	26.068	24.316	22.727	21.281	18.764	16.663	14.898	13.406	12.137	11.051	10.116	9.307	7.984	6.961	6.152	5.502	4.970
30	27.794	25.808	24.016	22.396	19.600	17.292	15.372	13.765	12.409	11.258	10.274	9.427	8.055	7.003	6.177	5.517	4.979
32	29.503	27.270	25.267	23.468	20.389	17.874	15.803	14.084	12.647	11.435	10.406	9.526	8.112	7.035	6.196	5.528	4.985
34	31.196	28.703	26.482	24.499	21.132	18.411	16.193	14.368	12.854	11.587	10.518	9.609	8.157	7.060	6.210	5.536	4.990
36	32.871	30.108	27.661	25.489	21.832	18.908	16.547	14.621	13.035	11.717	10.612	9.677	8.192	7.079	6.220	5.541	4.993
40	36.172	32.835	29.916	27.355	23.115	19.793	17.159	15.046	13.332	11.925	10.757	9.779	8.244	7.105	6.233	5.548	4.997
44	39.408	35.455	32.041	29.080	24.254	20.549	17.663	15.383	13.558	12.077	10.861	9.849	8.276	7.120	6.241	5.552	4.998
48	42.580	37.974	34.043	30.673	25.267	21.195	18.077	15.650	13.730	12.189	10.934	9.897	8.297	7.130	6.245	5.554	4.999

Index

About the Authors

G. EDDY BIRRER is Professor of Accounting and Assistant Dean of the School of Business Administration, Gonzaga University. He is the author of several publications on the subjects of accounting for bonds, leases, and pensions. In addition, Birrer has presented continuing professional education workshops to CPA firms and organizations on the use of present value applications, with special emphasis on lease accounting. Before entering the teaching profession, he worked on the audit staff of a Big Eight CPA firm.

JEAN L. CARRICA is Professor of Finance at Gonzaga University. His primary teaching fields are financial management and entrepreneurial planning. His prior publications cover topics such as entrepreneurship and business valuation. In addition to past experience as a business school dean, Carrica has served as an expert witness in wrongful death and injury lawsuits and as a board member of major corporations. His work history includes several years of successful small business ownership and management in the real estate industry.